SAUL A. RUBINSTEIN
THOMAS A. KOCHAN

LEARNING FROM SATURN:

Possibilities for Corporate Governance and Employee Relations

ILR Press
an imprint of
CORNELL UNIVERSITY PRESS
ITHACA AND LONDON

First published 2001 by Cornell University Press

Printed in the United States of America

Library of Congress Cataloging-in-Publication Data

Rubinstein, Saul A.
  Learning from Saturn / Saul A. Rubinstein and Thomas A. Kochan.
    p. cm.
Includes index.
  ISBN 0-8014-3873-X (cloth : alk. paper)
  1. Saturn Corporation. 2. Automobile industry and trade--United States. 3. Automobile industry and trade--Management--Employee Participation--United States. 4. International Union, United Automobile Workers of America (CIO) I. Kochan, Thomas A. II. Title.
  HD9710..U54 S277 2001
  338.7'629222'0973--dc21

00-011343

Cornell University Press strives to use environmentally responsible suppliers and materials to the fullest extent possible in the publishing of its books. Such materials include vegetable-based, low-VOC inks and acid-free papers that are recycled, totally chlorine-free, or partly composed of nonwood fibers. Books that bear the logo of the FSC (Forest Stewardship Council) use paper taken from forests that have been inspected and certified as meeting the highest standards for environmental and social responsibility. For further information, visit our website at www.cornellpress.cornell.edu.

Cloth printing 10 9 8 7 6 5 4 3 2 1

FSC FSC Trademark © 1996 Forest Stewardship Council A.C.
SW-COC-098

To the memory of Sidney P. Rubinstein, who worked throughout his life to make workplaces more democratic

Contents

Acknowledgments

We would like to thank the leaders of Saturn, General Motors (GM), and the United Auto Workers (UAW), who allowed us to observe and study their organizational experiment throughout what we refer to here as its first generation. The idea to embark on this project grew out of discussions in the early 1980s with Donald Ephlin and Alfred Warren. They were testing out ideas they hoped would eventually transform GM and the UAW. Later, Skip LeFauve, Saturn's chief executive officer from 1985 to 1996, and Michael Bennett, the leader of UAW Local 1853, encouraged us to provide an objective account of their experiences and to feed back our results in a timely fashion. More recently, Saturn's new CEO, Cynthia Trudell, and her management colleagues, particularly Nancy Brown-Johnston and Brian McClelland, as well as newly elected UAW leaders Jeep Williams and Ron Hankins, carried on this tradition by engaging us in a discussion of how to work with the conclusions and implications presented in Chapter 6. Throughout this time, we have been welcomed at Saturn and in the UAW, encouraged to talk with anyone we wished throughout their organizations, and accepted as independent researchers. We could not have asked for more.

Leaders at the corporate level of GM and the UAW International Union also listened to and discussed our results with us at various stages of the research. We thank GM Chief Executive Richard Wagoner, Vice President of Labor Relations Gary Cowger, and UAW Vice President Richard Shoemaker for their input and comments on this work.

In writing this book, we draw heavily on our more theoretical and technical analyses published in several academic journals. We thank the *Industrial and Labor Relations Review, Organization Science, Industrial Relations,* and the Industrial Relations Research Association for permission to draw on those works. Although our findings have been vetted by the normal academic peer review processes, here we sought to distill and extend them in a way that engages decision-makers who will shape the future of Saturn as well as others who will be designing organizations and labor relations systems in other settings.

Initial funding for this research was provided by the Massachusetts Institute of Technology (MIT) Leaders for Manufacturing Program and the MIT International Motor Vehicle Research Program. Later support was provided by the National Science Foundation's Program on Transformations to Quality Organizations and by the Alfred P. Sloan Foundation. These organizations made it possible for us to continue our work for an extended period without requesting or accepting funds from Saturn, GM, the UAW, or any other direct party of interest.

Phil Beaumont, Irving Bluestone, Adrienne Eaton, Don Ephlin, Charles Heckscher, Harry Katz, Doug Kruse, John Paul MacDuffie, and Robert McKersie read an earlier draft of this manuscript. Their comments were essential in helping us distinguish the forest from the trees in this endeavor. Iris Rubinstein patiently proofread and edited this manuscript with loving care. Susan Cass and Karen Boyajian at MIT and Amy Marchitto at Rutgers provided excellent and creative administrative support for this project. Among other things, they had to keep finding ways to pay for visits to the Steeplechase Inn in Spring Hill, Tennessee.

Finally, we want to thank the men and women of Saturn. We hope that this book conveys the tremendous pride, skill, and dedication they put into building a "Different Kind of Company and Different Kind of Car" on a daily basis.

LEARNING FROM SATURN: POSSIBILITIES FOR CORPORATE GOVERNANCE AND EMPLOYEE RELATIONS

What's at Stake Here?

The last two decades of the twentieth century will be recorded by
business and labor historians as a time of tumultuous change and
debate over two key issues: What goals should corporations serve,
and how should the system of labor-management relations be reformed?
Business historians will describe those years as ones in which shareholders
and investors sought to reassert control over corporations to increase
shareholder returns, while employees and other stakeholders sought a
greater voice in the issues that affected their jobs and long-term economic
security. At its core, this debate was about whether corporations
should focus on and be held accountable solely for maximizing shareholder
value or whether they should be conceived as more complex
institutions accountable to multiple stakeholders.[1]

Labor historians will mark the end of the twentieth century as the
time when academics and practitioners debated whether the system of
labor relations put in place in the 1930s as part of the New Deal had
run its course. Collective bargaining, the cornerstone of that system,
was under siege. Three different positions were staked out in this
debate. Some believed labor-management relations needed to be transformed
by introducing more flexible work systems and giving employees
more say over how to do their jobs and in the strategic management
decisions that shape the enterprise and long-term job security.[2] In the
absence of these changes, collective bargaining coverage and effectiveness
would continue to decline. Managers and union leaders who
shared this view introduced a wide range of innovations. Some
employers adopted an entirely different position by taking actions to

avoid any form of union representation. They intensified their opposition to unions and effectively kept them from organizing new work sites.[3] Finally, some union leaders and researchers argued that collective bargaining would withstand its temporary setbacks and make a comeback, particularly if labor law was changed to neutralize management's opposition.[4]

Historians will also note that these debates over the corporation and labor relations systems were not resolved by the end of the century.[5] So, as we enter the twenty-first century, the job of deciding the appropriate roles of shareholders and other stakeholders in corporate governance and the future of labor-management relations remains. In the years ahead, American managers, workers and their representatives, public policy makers, and ultimately the American public will need to decide what types of relationships between employees and managers and what forms of corporate governance are best suited to the needs of the economy and work force of this century.

To make effective choices, we need to learn from the experiments and innovations that emerged from the tumultuous environment of the 1980s and 1990s. This book examines the boldest and most far-reaching experiment in organizational form and labor-management relationship created in the last two decades: the Saturn Corporation. Saturn is unique because it embodies both a different model of organizational governance and a very different concept of labor-management relations. It therefore warrants a close look by those involved in both the debate over corporate governance and the debate over labor-management relations. Indeed, if the Saturn case does anything, it demonstrates that these two debates are inseparable and should be treated as one.

"A Different Kind of Company"

In 1983, General Motors Corporation (GM) and the United Auto Workers union (UAW) announced a bold new initiative: They would work together as partners to build a new small car in the United States using American suppliers and employing American workers represented by the UAW. This would truly fulfill the slogan "A Different Kind of Company and A Different Kind of Car." It was also to be a learning laboratory for the rest of GM as the company strived to regain market share and remake its image as the world's biggest and best automaker.

From 1992 to 1998, Saturn produced and marketed cars that achieved world-class quality and customer satisfaction unsurpassed by any other vehicle manufactured in the United States. Worldwide, only the Infiniti and the Lexus, two high-priced luxury cars selling for three to five times as much as the Saturn, received higher customer satisfaction ratings. On the surface, this proved to be a tremendous success for GM and the UAW, which finally demonstrated that the company and union could meet the challenge of international competition with world-class quality automobiles designed, sourced, and assembled domestically.

Yet, big concerns and uncertainties have clouded Saturn's future, and these prompt the questions: Has the Saturn experiment been successful? Is it seen as a failure, or perhaps a good idea for its time but irrelevant in the current industry environment? Was Saturn a "good investment" for GM? Is it profitable, and should it be expected to be profitable on its own? How was the remarkable quality performance achieved? Was Saturn a good idea for the UAW? How does its high level of participation in managerial affairs change the role of the union and its leaders? How should this union model fit into the strategy for the labor movement of the twenty-first century?

These questions are controversial and unresolved within GM's management and the UAW, and they are questions the American public cannot answer on the basis of public accounts and business press reports of Saturn's ups and downs. Still, they need to be answered, not only to set the record straight about Saturn but also to help us avoid reaching overly simplistic conclusions about what we can learn from Saturn.

To achieve world-class quality quickly—and in fact, exceed the levels achieved by its GM parent after only two years of production—Saturn used a new, locally designed manufacturing system that was built on self-directed teams and included the labor union as a full partner in business decisions. Its most unusual and controversial characteristic was the placement of hundreds of union representatives in the operations and staff management structure. Yet, over the years, Saturn's manufacturing organization in Spring Hill, Tennessee became increasingly isolated within the GM organization. Originally this was by design, because Saturn's creators believed it needed to be separated from the habits of its parents. Later, after its original champions had left GM and the UAW, Saturn's isolation continued not so much by conscious intent but because, as Saturn relished its image as "A Different Kind of Company and A Different Kind of Car," GM and the UAW national union turned their attention to their own battles and problems. Isolation and autonomy then were replaced by centralization, when GM sought to reintegrate Saturn's design and component sourcing decisions within the giant GM North American Operations Division as part of the overall corporate strategy for rationalizing its engineering design and sharing product platforms and components.

In 1996 GM, supported by the UAW's national leaders, decided to build the second-generation, somewhat larger and more upscale, Saturn model in GM's Wilmington, Delaware plant. From GM's and the UAW's viewpoint, this made sense because Wilmington was scheduled to close in a few years unless a new product was placed there. GM and the UAW went on, however, to build what was essentially a fire wall between Wilmington and Spring Hill. Few of the organizational and labor-management features of the original Saturn would be used in Wilmington, the car's design and engine would come from GM's German subsidiary, Opel; and sourcing of components would be done in a traditional GM fashion without union input. The labor-management system in the Wilmington Saturn plant would be covered under the national UAW-GM contract. The unions at Wilmington and Spring Hill were strongly discouraged and at times actively prevented from interacting with each other. Workers and union leaders at Spring Hill felt their future job security slipping away for lack of a product to replace Saturn's first model, lack of influence with GM and UAW decision makers, and lack of understanding and support for the lessons learned from the first generation of their unique partnership.

In the twenty-one months between April 1998 and December 1999, issues affecting the future of Saturn intensified. Saturn became a cauldron of conflict and change. In a series of rapid-fire developments,

- Union and company negotiators modified the risk-and-reward bonus system to try to reflect declining small-car sales and to realign the incentive formula to better reflect factors that workers and local officials could influence.
- The union issued a thirty-day strike notice—the first in its history— to create a deadline to force a decision over whether Spring Hill would get a second-generation product to build and to resolve continuing differences over the risk-and-reward formula.
- As part of the negotiated settlement, GM agreed to consider building a Saturn sport utility vehicle (SUV) in Spring Hill if the parties could make the case to produce it efficiently and profitably.

- GM appointed a new CEO for Saturn, Cynthia Trudell, a highly respected manager with significant experience leading manufacturing operations in Europe and North America, including a tour of duty at the Wilmington plant before it became part of Saturn.
- Rank-and-file union members at Spring Hill voted to replace the entire slate of incumbent union leaders with a team that promised to continue the partnership but to be more responsive to members' concerns.
- Rank-and-file union members at Wilmington voted to replace the shop chairwoman, who had vigorously opposed any form of labor-management partnership, with a leader committed to building an effective joint process.
- Saturn management and union representatives agreed on a plan for building the SUV that gained GM's approval and authorization of the needed capital.
- Saturn management and union leadership embarked on a joint study process to figure out how to renew and carry the partnership and the "Different Kind of Company and Car" spirit into its second generation.
- After the national negotiations between the UAW and GM, negotiations were held between the UAW and Saturn. Among the issues of concern raised were the risk-and-reward bonus system, election versus selection of union representatives, shift rotation, and the relationship to the national GM agreement.
- Although negotiations concluded with some modifications to the risk-and-reward formula and the addition of six elected union representatives, the basic Saturn agreement remained intact and was ratified by 89 percent.

Saturn is struggling to enter its second generation as an innovative organization with a successful track record and renewed determination and spirit. Significant challenges lie ahead, however. Unless all the parties at Saturn, GM, and the UAW learn from their first-generation experience and use these lessons to shape its future, Saturn may fail or, at a minimum, many of its distinctive features may erode and revert back to their traditional form.

We believe that would be a mistake and a sad result not only for GM, its workers and shareholders, and the UAW, but also for the nation. It would ensure that both the private and public returns on the investments made in

Saturn are never realized. As Lynn Williams, former president of the United Steelworkers, said, "It would be a terrible shame if Saturn fails—it would signal an enormous setback for efforts many of us have made to change the course of labor relations in America. We all have a stake in Saturn's success."

It is not too late to learn and act on the lessons to reposition Saturn for the next generation of its contributions to GM and the UAW. Nor is it too late for leaders in labor, business, and government to learn from Saturn and use these lessons to get on with the task of updating labor-management and corporate governance policies to better fit the needs of the economy and society of the twenty-first century.

To this end, our book is essentially an extended memo to everyone with a stake in Saturn. This includes, but goes well beyond, the employees and managers at Saturn and its GM and UAW parents. Saturn's customers and retailers bought the entire package–a different kind of company *and* a different kind of car. The American public, particularly those people concerned about the future of labor-management relations in the United States, has a big stake in learning from Saturn as well. As Williams pointed out, Saturn has been a beacon in an otherwise dark era for labor relations in America. When the company was created, it promised to serve as a learning laboratory for a new partnership model from which labor, management, and government policy makers might learn. The fact that its experience was controversial makes it no less important or valuable to learn the right lessons from this experience. Like most organizational innovations, Saturn's story is neither an unqualified success nor a complete failure. We need to assess its basic strengths and limitations as a model for the future of unions, labor-management relations, work organization, and corporate governance in America. That means looking at it openly, critically, and in depth. That's what we hope to do in this book.

We write as academics who have had the good fortune to work closely with labor and management leaders at Saturn since its inception. Our relationship dates to the early 1980s, when our industrial relations group at the Massachusetts Institute of Technology (MIT) was researching the tumultuous changes occurring in labor-management relations during that decade.[6] In the process, we came to know Don Ephlin and Al Warren, leaders of the UAW and GM, respectively, who were the original champions and architects of Saturn. We shared their basic view that more participative and flexible approaches to labor relations were needed throughout the entire organization—from the shop floor to the inner workings of strategic decision making—to transform the American labor relations system. After

Saturn was launched, we were encouraged by its management and labor leaders—Saturn President Richard "Skip" LeFauve and Local Union President Mike Bennett—to track the Saturn experiences in order to provide an independent assessment of the successes and failures along the way and to create a record from which interested parties could learn. As our work at Spring Hill unfolded, we continued to serve as outside researchers, but from time to time we also became partners with labor and management in solving problems and designing training based on the results of our work.

Saul Rubinstein, while at MIT, wrote his Ph.D. dissertation on Saturn and spent countless hours on the shop floor and in meetings with key management and labor leaders, gathering data and, when opportunities arose, providing feedback on how to make their structures and processes work more effectively. When Saul took a faculty position at Rutgers University, we continued our collaboration with Saturn and hosted a series of training seminars and workshops for Saturn's leaders. At the invitation of LeFauve, we met with a group that called itself the "Saturn Alumni," GM managers who had worked for a time at Saturn and transferred back to GM, and analyzed what they learned from applying partnership principles back in the parent environment. In 1999 we were invited by the new management and union leaders at Spring Hill and Wilmington to facilitate a process whereby they could accelerate learning from Saturn's past, as well as increase learning from each other across organizational boundaries.

This, then, is the story of the company and the union as we have observed it over its first decade-and-a-half, and it draws out the lessons of this experience for the future of U.S. labor relations and the future of the American corporation. We explore what worked at Saturn, what didn't, and why it is so difficult to spread the real lessons of this unique experiment within its parent organizations and across American industry.

Confusing Debates

A New Labor Relations Model

Saturn represents the most radical experiment with a new labor relations model in the United States and, indeed, perhaps in the world. The traditional American labor relations model grew out of the laws passed as part of the New Deal in the 1930s and the large-scale corporate organizational forms that dominated American industry throughout most of the twentieth century. By the early 1980s, however, it was becoming clear that this model no longer worked for either employers or workers and their unions. Management needed greater flexibility, more cooperation and involvement from the work force, and higher quality and productivity. Unions needed a new strategy for organizing workers (and especially needed to neutralize employer opposition to organizing), a new role and source of power, and access to the levels of management at which the key strategic decisions influencing worker welfare were being made. Moreover, workers were calling for a greater say in the decisions affecting their jobs and work environment and at the same time demanding more assurances of job security from their unions and their employers.

These pressures sparked a decade of conflict, struggle, and innovation in labor relations. No industry other than automaking and no company other than GM was more at the center of both the conflicts and the innovations.[7] From 1973, beginning at its Tarrytown, New York assembly plant, GM began experimenting with quality of working life (QWL) off-line (away from the point of production) efforts to involve employees in problem-solving groups. From QWL, GM moved to experimentation with on-line (as part of the regular production process), self-directed work teams in plants such as its Pontiac Fiero facility and then its joint venture with Toyota—the New United Motors Manufacturing Inc. (NUMMI). Saturn followed these efforts and built on their successes and limitations. But Saturn went well beyond these innovations and designed its organizational and labor-management system from scratch. NUMMI and other earlier innovations in labor-management relations focused on changing practices and relations on the shop floor but kept intact the traditional principle that it was management's job to make the strategic and operational decisions. The designers of Saturn challenged this principle. Labor and management would work in partnership at all levels of the organization—from the shop floor to the highest levels of managerial decision making. As a result of this radical departure, Saturn presents a case study of an alternative and highly controversial labor relations model. Given the recognition that the traditional model no longer works, it is important that we draw the right lessons—the strengths and weaknesses—from experiences of the Saturn alternative.

A New Organizational Model

The organizational principles embedded in Saturn challenge fundamental doctrines guiding the legal structure and theory of the American corporation. Saturn's original purposes, organizational design, governance structures, and internal processes embody the features many envision for a company that seeks to satisfy the goals of multiple stakeholders. In contrast, American companies are charged by law and structure with maximizing the interests of one set of stakeholders—the shareholders—over all others. Saturn, however, was set up with dual objectives—to make small cars profitably (and thus provide a return to GM shareholders) *and* to create (or retain) good jobs for American workers and UAW members. Its definition of good jobs included increased influence over important decisions. Moreover, as is seen in later chapters, Saturn's design reflects many of the principles others have argued are key to responding to the needs of other stakeholders as well, particularly retailers and suppliers. For example, from the beginning, Saturn treated its retailers (dealers) as partners by involving them in decision making and choosing a distribution strategy designed to produce above-average profits per car for the retailers. Similarly, by choosing a single-source supplier strategy rather than one in which multiple suppliers would continuously compete against each other on the basis of price, Saturn sought to build long-term partnerships with these stakeholders.

Today we hear calls from many quarters for firms to respond more directly to their shareholders and to other stakeholders. Indeed, shareholders and their agents became an increasing force in corporate decision making in the late 1980s and 1990s, demanding higher and more immediate returns on their investments.[8] With respect to employees, there is a growing concern that the basic social contract at work has been broken by the downsizing, outsourcing, and restructuring firms have undergone in response to increased shareholder pressures, global competition, and changing technologies.[9] We need to look at Saturn with an eye toward learning what might be done to manage the internal processes and external relationships of a firm that seeks to achieve a better balance of the needs and goals of multiple stakeholders. Ultimately, the question is this: Can such a firm survive in the U.S. environment, where maximizing shareholder value enjoys such a privileged status?

Saturn embodies many of the features organizational theorists have in mind when they describe a "networked organization."[10] Networked organizations are expected to depart from traditional bureaucracies and hierarchies by relying more heavily on multiple horizontal communication links for coordination and problem solving. In traditional bureaucratic organizations, hierarchy and formal authority relationships are expected to serve these coordination and communication functions. Networked organizations are expected to be especially effective in settings in which information is dispersed among multiple parties inside and outside the formal structure or organizational boundaries, and flexibility, adaptability, and problem solving among different groups or stakeholders are important. In these situations, networks add value to the organization by producing "social capital"–that is, the ability to get things done or help individuals solve problems by linking people who have the information and power needed to make things happen.[11]

Saturn was not consciously designed to be a networked organization. Few organizations are. The ties needed to build informal communications networks tend to evolve when other conditions support them, such as when there are many social, political, or task-related opportunities that bring people together and produce new contacts, friendships, political coalitions, and reputations as good sources of information and expertise. At Saturn the partnership structures and processes that the union and the company put in place had exactly these unanticipated but positive consequences. If networked features are as important to the fast-paced economy of the future as many believe them to be, a close look at how Saturn evolved to become a highly networked organization is indeed warranted.

"A Different Kind of Union"

We make no bones about it. We believe in the need for strong, innovative, democratic unions in America. Yet America has allowed its labor movement to decline to the point at which the capacity of union leaders to be innovative and forward looking is subverted by the need to fight for survival. This must change, and the union at Saturn has lessons for the labor unions of the future. These ideas need to be debated within the labor movement and among policy makers and those in industry who share our view that a viable labor movement is an essential bulwark of a democratic society and an economy that aspires to achieve a broadly shared prosperity.[12] Unions, however, cannot meet their historic obligations to workers and society by clinging to or hoping for a return to what made them successful in the past. At Saturn, the local union has created its own dense social network that builds a broad base of leadership and participation, contributes to the performance of the enterprise, and derives bargaining power from its new role. Leaders and rank-and-file members in this local union are developing the capacity to share in the problem solving, management, and governance of the enterprise—skills and capabilities we see as essential to securing workers' long-term careers in the new economy and adding value to their enterprises and the national economy. But carrying out these different roles generates a new set of internal tensions and conflicts in relations with the national union. The union at Saturn is a window on the issues that a different kind of union must confront and manage if the labor movement is to be revitalized to fulfill its historic functions for workers and society.

What Follows

In the chapters that follow, we provide the detailed information needed to make informed judgments about what to learn from this experiment in labor relations and organizational design. We start by placing Saturn in its proper historical perspective by tracing its organizing principles back to the vision of the legendary UAW leader Walter Reuther. Then we explore the inner workings of Saturn and the local union over their first generation of experience, focusing on the co-management process and on the unique features introduced by the local union in its attempts to balance its role in the partnership with its role on the shop floor. Then we turn to the challenges associated with managing the external boundaries between Saturn and its UAW and GM parents.

Finally, we draw on this information to suggest what we believe are the right lessons to learn from Saturn's first-generation experience and how these lessons can be applied beyond the organizational boundaries of GM and the UAW. Lessons from Saturn may have had limited success in penetrating the fortress-like walls of GM and the UAW. However, we can learn from Saturn's achievements and failures in our efforts to shape labor-management policy and transform the American corporation to achieve a better social contract among workers, customers, shareholders, and the broader society. Ultimately, these are the most important lessons that Saturn offers.

2

Walter Reuther's Legacy: The Ideas behind Saturn

I n 1945 Walter Reuther, the most innovative labor leader of the post-war generation, led the UAW on a strike against GM. To settle it, he proposed a grand bargain: Union members would hold the line on wages if the company agreed to hold the line on prices. Part of the bargain would require, not surprisingly, that GM open its books. If union members were to tie their fate more directly to the success or failure of the company, union representatives would need a stronger voice in the management of the firm.

GM rejected these demands, viewing them as infringements on their managerial prerogatives. Eventually, under pressure from his counterparts in the steel industry, Reuther settled for a wage increase patterned after the one agreed to in that industry. But Reuther continued to talk about the need for worker input. In response to a similar demand in 1948, GM's chairman, Charles Wilson, offered what turned out to be the historic bargain that would shape the wage-setting process in the auto industry for the next several decades and close the door to direct involvement of workers or their unions in managerial decision making. He proposed to increase wages in tandem with increases in the cost of living and productivity improvements. The mold for labor relations in the auto industry and, indeed, for postwar industrial relations in America, was set. Management would negotiate incremental improvements that would raise workers' standards of living in tandem with increases in the productivity and overall economic trends, and, in return, unions would stay out of management's affairs.[1] Reflecting on the opportunities closed off by this bargain, Irving Bluestone, a UAW colleague of Reuther and later the vice president of the UAW in charge of the GM department, and his son Barry wrote:

> For all practical purposes, the major battle over management rights in strategic decisions was over by the end of the 1940s. Unions had cemented the right to co-manage vital workplace issues, but corporate executives retained the sole right to manage the enterprise. This separation of control has continued, more or less intact, to the present day.[2]

Postwar Social Contract

Reuther and the UAW went on to introduce to employment contracts many innovative features that both union and nonunion workers in America now take for granted. Among these were generous pensions and the famous thirty-and-out early retirement plan; supplementary unemployment benefits to cushion the cyclical downturns expected in the industry; and paid time off not just for vacations, but a decade before its time, paid personal leave for family needs or personal business or recreation. Other innovations included jointly funded training programs, safety and health committees, and many more aspects of what we now refer to nostalgically as the old social contract, in which workers shared in the prosperity of their companies and the overall economy.

But by the 1970s cracks were appearing in this labor relations mold. First, workers began to rebel against the boredom of work on the assembly line. Wildcat strikes, such as the one in 1972 at GM's giant Lordstown, Ohio, assembly facility, were widely read as a sign of the blue-collar blues. Right or wrong (and according to Irving Bluestone, the UAW vice president involved directly in this case, it was the wrong interpretation—the strike was really about an old-fashioned speed-up of the assembly line), a national debate was born: Were blue-collar workers alienated by factory work, and was there some way to change their experiences to improve their QWL?[3]

Efforts to address QWL issues were obviously not new. In fact, a number of nonunion companies had been quietly experimenting with new approaches to managing the work force throughout the 1960s, practicing job enrichment or job rotation and working hard to improve relations between workers and supervisors and thereby overcome the adversarial, low-trust climate of the workplace. Unfortunately, this process gained a bad name in a number of union-management circles because it was perceived, with considerable justification, as a ploy to avoid unions. By satisfying workers' needs for involvement and treating workers with more respect, the motivation to unionize would decline. Any militancy within the work force would be reduced, and if necessary, the traditional hardball tactics for dealing with these dissidents and their union activity could be more easily applied.

QWL was no better received by traditional labor relations executives. In fact, one of the most vigorous opponents to using social-psychological, or "soft," theories and practices to manage the work force was the then vice president of labor relations at GM, George Morris. His view, shared by the majority of his labor relations executive colleagues of the 1960s and early 1970s, was that labor relations was his turf and he knew how to deal with union representatives. Anyone foolish enough to try to tread on his turf or deal with workers directly at the workplace did so at his or her own peril and would simply threaten to mess up a well-functioning labor-management system.

Despite this rocky start, calls for experimentation with QWL persisted and, in fact, grew steadily within the auto industry. By 1973 the power struggle within GM management had built up enough support for QWL that a provision was included in the national GM-UAW agreement to set up a company-union committee to oversee QWL experiments. Also in 1973, the first major experiment in GM at the Tarrytown, New York assembly plant was begun and later reported as a great success,[4] as indeed it was. An otherwise old and somewhat antiquated plant was kept viable and functioning for another twenty years. Thus, the QWL movement gained its initial foothold within GM, the UAW, and the auto industry.

QWL efforts grew sporadically through the 1970s in GM facilities as different managers and local union leaders took it upon themselves to experiment with various forms of employee involvement. But it was the economic crisis that befell the U.S. auto industry in 1979 and 1980 that produced an acceleration and broadening of the experimentation. In 1979 the National Broadcasting Company (NBC) produced a news special titled "If Japan Can, Why Can't We?" The question was this: What made Japanese manufacturers in general, and the Japanese auto industry in particular, appear to be so productive and to have surpassed the United States in their ability to produce high-quality vehicles? The combination of the deep recession, high oil prices, availability of cheaper and higher-quality Japanese imported cars, and, later in the 1980s, Japanese cars manufactured in the United States, demonstrated the need for more fundamental changes in U.S. labor relations and management systems.

The need for major change was clearly brought home to the industry and those of us who studied it in the 1980s by three sets of data: (1) evidence of the costs associated with the traditional labor-management relations model, (2) the failed efforts to solve the problem with stand-alone technological solutions, and (3) the results of the experiment called NUMMI.

Costs of Traditional Adversarial Relations

In the early 1980s, our Massachusetts Institute of Technology (MIT) industrial relations research group uncovered a body of data that would have a profound effect on our thinking about the need for change in traditional industrial relations. With data collected from GM plants by two graduate students working under the supervision of our colleague Harry Katz, we discovered the wide variation in productivity and quality performance in GM's facilities and the impact that variations in industrial relations practices and activities had on productivity and quality. In a series of quantitative studies, we found that productivity varied more than 100 percent across different GM plants, even though all these plants were governed by the same labor agreements, used roughly the same general technologies and methods of production, and employed the same management systems.[5] What accounted for these differences? Unfortunately, for advocates of QWL, it was not simply the amount of QWL activity under way in the plants. (We originally conducted these studies to assess the effects of QWL on productivity and quality, but as it turned out, our other findings were much more informative.) QWL did help to increase quality, but we could find no effect on productivity aside from the indirect effect that plants with more worker participation required fewer supervisors and therefore managerial costs were lower. Instead, the larger portion of the variation in performance was explained by the extent to which the labor-management system and the work organization arrangements produced and reinforced a cycle of high conflict and low trust which then produced more ˙k rules and grievances over the enforcement of these rules.

wo conclusions flowed from these results. First, the traditional indus-relations system in these plants was not productive and needed to be changed. Second, QWL interventions alone were not enough to make the difference in the plants. More fundamental change was needed.

GM and the UAW had quietly begun to experiment with bolder modifications to the production system—bringing in team concepts to organize work and reducing the number of job classifications and the complexity of the work rules governing labor relations. Again, this movement was controversial within the union because GM's first experience with team systems occurred when they opened several plants in the South on a nonunion basis—their so-called Southern strategy. Although the UAW eventually forced GM to abandon its nonunion strategy and these plants became unionized, the link between teams and antiunionism was cemented in the minds of some union leaders and rank-and-file members. Overcoming this legacy through joint union-management efforts to introduce and oversee team systems in organized plants was not easy.

Several plants, however, did just that. The Pontiac Fiero manufacturing plant in Ohio was perhaps the most highly publicized example of a successful team-concept plant in the GM system. Alas, the Fiero (a small, fiberglass-body mid-engine sports car) was a bust in the marketplace. Even though the union leaders in that plant, backed by top UAW officers, had taken the risks of supporting the team concept and had demonstrated its value to the company and to the rank and file, GM decided to close the plant. This decision sent shock waves through the union with a message that undermined the political position of advocates of innovation: GM doesn't really care about these issues. Only profit matters.

The High-Technology Solution

The second big lesson came from the failure of GM's $50 billion adventure into high technology. Some in GM management had another answer to NBC's question. Yes, the U.S. industry could do it too, but in its own way—with heavy investment in the most advanced technology money could buy. GM was the poster child for this strategy in the 1980s. Over the decade, GM spent more than $50 billion on advanced technologies in its plants. We visited some of these, such as the Hamtramck facility in Michigan, the Linden plant in New Jersey, and the Wilmington, Delaware plant (later to become a Saturn facility). In these plants, one could see the wizardry and complexity of the automated tracking systems that guided parts to their appropriate spot on the assembly line and the robots. Too often, however, the robots stood idle, were under repair, or in some cases were moved off the assembly line to allow workers to get the job done the old-fashioned way. As a result, GM learned a lesson, one that two MIT students would later quantify[6]: a company can't find its way to the highest levels of productivity and quality simply by automating inferior systems. At the end of the decade, after spending $50 billion, GM was still the highest-cost car manufacturer in America.

NUMMI and Its Legacy

The third body of data that influenced decision makers in the auto industry, far more than the data that opened our eyes to the need for change, was the performance of NUMMI, a joint venture between GM and Toyota set up in 1982 to produce compact cars for both companies. Toyota was to manage the new organization in a former GM plant in Fremont, California that had been shut down two years earlier. Fremont had a reputation as one of GM's worst plants in terms of productivity, quality, and labor relations.

The NUMMI story is so much a part of industrial folklore in the auto industry that we need only to summarize its outcome here.[7] The plant was restarted using Toyota's management, production system, and labor relations, but retaining the same union leaders, largely the same work force, and the same relatively old technology. Within two years it had become the most productive and highest-quality auto producer in the United States. The data displayed in Table 2-1 illustrate this finding. This table was generated by John Krafcik's research at the MIT International Motor Vehicle Research Program for his master's thesis in 1988. We used this table numerous times in courses for senior executives at MIT, some of whom were from GM or other parts of the auto industry. Showing these data reinforced the notion that a picture is worth a thousand words. Time and again, executives who were skeptical about the power of high trust and participative, flexible, secure, well-trained and properly led workers accepted the reality: positive labor relations, when combined with a production system that emphasized quality, flexibility and continuous learning, and integrated technology and human resources, could produce in the United States what Krafcik called "world-class manufacturing." This is what Paul Adler called a "learning bureaucracy,"[8] and what later (unfortunately) was labeled "lean production."

Table 2-1. NUMMI Compared with Other Auto Plants (1986)

Plant	Productivity[a] (Hrs/Unit)	Quality[b] (Defects/100 Units)	Automation Level[c] (0 = None)
Honda, Ohio	19.2	72.0	77.0
Nissan, Tennessee	24.5	70.0	89.2
NUMMI, California	19.0	69.0	62.8
Toyota, Japan	15.6	63.0	79.6
GM, Michigan	33.7	137.4	100.0
GM, Massachusetts	34.2	116.5	7.3

[a]Productivity = standardized number of man hours to weld, paint, and assemble a vehicle.
[b]Quality = defects attributable to assembly operations reported in first six months of ownership.
[c]Automation level = robotic applications/production rate, normalized to 100 for highest level in group.
Source: John Krafcik, Triumph of the Lean Production System, *Sloan Management Review*, 1988, Vol. 3, pp. 144–52.

NUMMI was intended to be a learning environment for GM. Although it never lived up to its billing as a learning laboratory that produced change within GM's North American management, it did have one big effect: it bolstered the conviction of UAW leaders Don Ephlin and Doug Fraser and GM Labor Relations Vice President Al Warren that big benefits were to be had if they could replicate the NUMMI results in GM's own operations. The distant glow of Saturn was beginning to shine through the mist. In fact, discussions of the Saturn concept were beginning as the negotiations to arrange the joint venture at NUMMI were being completed.

Saturn and the Committee of 99

In the early 1980s, GM was importing most of its compact cars from Japan, because its own engineering studies had concluded it could not manufacture small cars competitively in the United States under the existing labor relations and management systems. Therefore, GM approached the UAW International with a proposal for a joint study to investigate whether an alternative system was possible. A joint union-management committee was formed and charged with evaluating the key success factors of world-class manufacturing. The Committee of 99, as the joint study team came to be called, started with a clean sheet and explored best practices worldwide.[9]

The committee benchmarked operations around the world, inside and outside the auto industry. It established seven benchmarking subcommittees: (1) stamping; (2) metal fabrication and body shops; (3) paint and corrosion; (4) engine and transmission; (5) chassis; (6) trim, hardware, and assembly; and (7) electrical, heating, and cooling.

Members traveled to Europe to examine the socio-technical models of work organization found in the Uddevalla, Sweden and Kalmar, Sweden plants of Volvo. They went to Japan to get a firsthand look at the Toyota production system and the Japanese approaches to labor-management consultation, visiting, among others, Honda and Fuji Heavy Industries. Among North American companies benchmarked were 3M, Chrysler, Cummins Diesel, Dana, Donnelly Mirrors, Ford, GE Locomotive, General Foods, Herman Miller, Hitachi, Honda, Hyatt Clark, IBM, Kawasaki Motor Cycles, Lincoln Electric, MacDonald's, Motorola, NCR, Nissan, Nucor Steel, Prab Robotics, Procter & Gamble, Remington Rand, Sanyo, Sony, Toshiba, Upjohn Pharmaceuticals, Volkswagon, and Xerox. Further, the committee benchmarked more than thirty GM assembly and component parts plants, including Tarrytown, Fiero, Lordstown, and NUMMI, as well as GM dealers. In addition, members visited Harvard University, the University of Michigan, Michigan State University, Wayne State University, the University of Alabama, and the Illinois Institute of Technology.

Then, according to the account of committee member Jack O'Toole, members returned home and debated what they learned from these trips and how to adapt these lessons to address the multiple objectives they were given—to create an organization and labor-management relationship that could be successful for both the corporation and its represented work force.[10] As a result, although making extensive use of self-directed work teams, the committee did not copy the lean production model of Toyota or NUMMI but rather conceived a form of organizational governance that would enable management and the local union to jointly manage the business and that sought to achieve high quality and productivity while also addressing the key concerns of other stakeholders.

Its findings were the basis for Saturn's organizing principles, which appeared in 1985 as the twenty-eight–page Memorandum of Agreement between the UAW International and the Saturn Corporation. The Memo outlined not only the underlying principles of the partnership (Figure 2-1), but also the team and committee structure (Figure 2-2).

The decision to create Saturn met with opposition from both GM and the UAW. Within the corporation, the strongest supporters of the concept were CEO Roger Smith and Al Warren. Support for Saturn does not appear to have come from key operations managers, who believed GM could have better invested its resources in the existing divisions. Although one of Saturn's goals (see mission statement below) was to transfer learning back to GM, few managers seemed interested in disseminating this model of management and partnership.

- Treat people as a fixed asset. Provide opportunities for them to maximize their contributions and value to the organization. Provide extensive training and skill development to all employees.

- The Saturn organization will be based on groups which will attempt to identify and work collaboratively toward common goals.

- Saturn will openly share all information including financial data.

- Decision making will be based on consensus through a series of formal joint labor-management committees, or Decision Rings. As a stakeholder in the operation of Saturn the UAW will participate in business decisions as a full Partner including site selection and construction, process and product design, choice of technologies, supplier selection, make-buy decisions, retail dealer selection, pricing, business planning, training, business systems development, budgeting, quality systems, productivity improvement, job design, new product development, recruitment and hiring, maintenance, and engineering. However, GM would retain discretion over investment and new product decisions.

- Self-managed teams or Work Units will be the basic building blocks of the organization.

- Decision making authority will be located at the level of the organization where the necessary knowledge resides, and where implementation takes place. Emphasis will be placed on the work unit.

- There will be a minimum of job classifications.

- Saturn will have a jointly developed and administered recruitment and selection process, and work units will hire their own team members. Seniority will not be the basis for selection, and the primary recruiting pool will consist of active and laid off GM/UAW employees.

- The technical and social work organization will be integrated.

- There will be fewer full time elected UAW Officials and fewer Labor Relations personnel responsible for contract administration.

- Saturn's reward system will be designed to encourage everyone's efforts toward the common goals of quality, cost, timing, and value to the customer.

Figure 2-1. Saturn's Organizing Principles. (Source: Memorandum of Agreement, Saturn Corporation, 1985.)

- **Work Units** are organized into teams of 6 to 15 members, electing their own leaders who remain working members of the unit. They are self-directed and empowered with the authority, responsibility, and resources necessary to meet their day to day assignments and goals, including producing to budget, quality, housekeeping, safety and health, maintenance, material and inventory control, training, job assignments, repairs, scrap control, vacation approvals, absenteeism, supplies, record keeping, personnel selection and hiring, work planning, and work scheduling.

- Saturn has no supervisors in the traditional sense. Teams interrelated by geography, product, or technology are organized into modules. Modules have a common **Advisor**.

- Modules are integrated into three **Business Units**: Body Systems (stamping, body fabrication, injection molding, and paint); Powertrain (lost foam casting, machining and assembly of engines and transmissions), and Vehicle Systems (vehicle interior, chassis, hardware, trim, exterior panels and assembly).

- Joint Labor-Management **Decision Rings** meet weekly:

  - At the corporate level the **Strategic Action Council** (SAC) concerns itself with company-wide long range planning, and relations with dealers, suppliers, stockholders, and the community. Participating in the SAC for the union are the local president and UAW national representative.

  - The **Manufacturing Action Council** (MAC) covers the Spring Hill manufacturing and assembly complex. On the MAC representing the local are the union president, the MAC adviser, and the four vice presidents who also serve as the UAW bargaining committee.

  - Each **Business Unit** has a joint labor-management **Decision Ring** at the plant level. Executive board members are joined by UAW module advisors and crew coordinators in representing the union.

  - **Decision Rings** are also organized at the **Module** level. Module advisors and the elected work unit counselors (team leaders) participate in the module decision rings.

Figure 2-2. Saturn Partnership Structure.

Similarly, Saturn stimulated debate within the executive board of the UAW. The most controversial issues were Saturn's risk-and-reward compensation plan, a job security provision that covered only 80 percent of the membership, and the complete rotation of jobs and shifts. Some union leaders believed that (1) the risk-and-reward system linking pay to performance was a return to piecework, (2) the job security provision created two classes of employees, and (3) the rotation of jobs and shifts eliminated some of the long-sought benefits of job classifications and seniority. In all these areas—compensation plans, job security, seniority rights, and job classifications—the Saturn contract did not follow the national pattern. From the union's viewpoint, these variances could lead to whipsawing or the undermining of national pattern bargaining with the industry. Although the executive board ultimately approved the project after a two-day debate, opposition remained strong among a number of key leaders, who have continued to oppose exporting the model to other plants. Opposition also continued from the members of the dissident "New Directions" caucus, which included Reuther's brother Victor, who argued that the Saturn approach would erode the union's ability to represent its members by aligning the leadership too closely with management's interests. Leaders of this caucus also argued that the extensive use of teams would undermine the local union and increase the pressure on individual members.

With the approval of the UAW and the commitment of capital by the GM board, Saturn was born in 1985. What remained to be done was to translate the broad vision of a "different kind of company" into a functioning organization and labor-management relationship. During the period from 1985 to the time the first car rolled off the assembly line, the vision was translated from a blueprint, a twenty-eight–page labor agreement, to an ongoing working partnership between labor and management.

Saturn chose Spring Hill, Tennessee as the location for its manufacturing facilities. Spring Hill is a small farming community in the rolling hills of Tennessee, approximately forty miles south of Nashville. It constructed a fully integrated 4.2 million square foot facility, including a foundry, an engine and transmission plant, an assembly plant, and departments for stamping, body fabrication, and interior parts manufacturing. Saturn's engineering center is located in Troy, Michigan. Originally, GM planned to invest $5 billion to cover product development costs as well as construction of the new facilities and purchase of the needed equipment. Later, the amount was scaled down to $3 billion when GM experienced its financial crisis in the early 1990s.

Key Features of the Saturn Partnership

Memorandum of Agreement

Saturn Philosophy

We believe that all people want to be involved in decisions that affect them, care about their job and each other, take pride in themselves and in their contributions, and want to share in the success of their efforts.

The Saturn philosophy statement is the first part of the collective bargaining contract, the Memorandum of Agreement, governing the labor-management relationship.

For anyone used to reading standard collective bargaining agreements, the Saturn Memorandum of Agreement would have seemed to be a document in a foreign language. Unlike the precise rules governing rights and obligations of the parties found in the more than 400 pages of the GM-UAW national agreement, most of the language of the twenty-eight–page Saturn document stated principles to which the parties committed to follow and hold each other accountable. The philosophy statement is one example. Another unique feature of the agreement is the inclusion of Saturn's mission statement:

Saturn Mission Statement

The Mission of Saturn is to market vehicles developed and manufactured in the United States that are world leaders in quality, cost, and consumer satisfaction through the integration of people, technology, and business systems and to transfer knowledge, technology, and experience throughout General Motors Corporation.

The agreement committed the parties to an employment relationship that would meet the high industry benefits and labor standards achieved through years of hard bargaining and economic prosperity; however, the parties would get to these standards, in some cases, in different ways. Wages paid as salary were pegged to a percentage of the UAW-GM negotiated rate. The amount bringing wages to the GM level would be put at risk and depend on whether certain performance criteria—to be chosen later—would be met. An additional reward above the base rate was also to be achievable, again based on performance targets to be negotiated later. Thus, what the parties later referred to as the "risk-and-reward" pay plan was born. Job security was to be guaranteed for a minimum of 80 percent of the work force with the most seniority, barring "unforeseen or catastrophic events or severe economic conditions." This flat statement was something Reuther and his colleagues sought and never achieved in the 1940s. But unlike the national contract, the comprehensive array of specific job security provisions—supplemental unemployment benefits pay, transfer of rights if the plant closed, seniority bumping rights in the event of layoffs, and so forth—was absent. Thus, it was an all-or-nothing bet on the part of both Saturn and the work force. As long as Saturn survived, the workers would be guaranteed their jobs. If Saturn failed, however, the union members could not transfer back to other parts of GM, because they would have given up their seniority rights by joining Saturn.

Another departure, one we focus on in later chapters, involved the structure of work to be used in the bargaining unit. Building on the innovations with team-based work systems at Fiero, NUMMI, Toyota, Honda, and a growing number of other plants (especially new facilities) around the world, Saturn adopted the team as the basic work unit rather than the individual job classifications common to older plants established in an earlier era. There would be one production job classification and only six classifications for skilled trades employees.

Team members would rotate through all the jobs covered by the team's responsibilities, including many that were included in supervisory positions in the rest of GM. Teams would have leaders and would be linked together in modules (departments) that were led by represented and non-represented advisors who co-managed as partners. Further, no production or maintenance workers would work fixed shifts; instead, all three crews would rotate between day and night shifts.

In summary, the 1985 Saturn agreement embodied state-of-the-art thinking about what was required for world-class manufacturing and world-class jobs that used workers' full knowledge, commitment, and skills. But what is more striking about this labor agreement than its specific terms and conditions are the tone and the language used to convey the principles of mutual trust and respect that the parties hoped to build into their relationship through principles of joint consensus-based decision making, voluntary acceptance of the union as a partner in the organization, and a shared vision of what a world-class company and employment relationship of the 1980s should be.

Organizational Governance

Aside from the provisions for work teams, consensus principles, and joint decision making, the agreement also established several organizational structures for shared decision making at different levels. Specifically, it called for the local union to be a full partner in all business decisions (with the important exceptions of investment and new product decisions, issues that, as we will see, became critical as the organization evolved) and for the organization to be governed by joint labor-management committees (decision rings) at all levels—corporate (Strategic Action Council or SAC), manufacturing (Manufacturing Action Council or MAC), business unit (plant), and module.

The partnership organization and the structure of the local union have evolved to extend significantly beyond this basic blueprint. Figure 2-3 illustrates the evolved practices at Saturn in terms of four cells, the framework we use to analyze these arrangements and compare Saturn's joint governance system to other models of joint labor-management

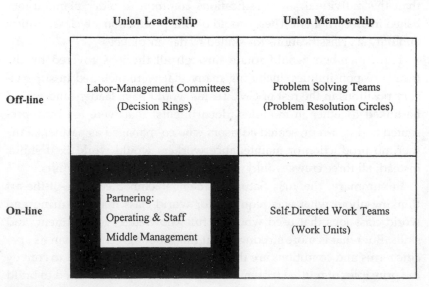

	Union Leadership	Union Membership
Off-line	Labor-Management Committees (Decision Rings)	Problem Solving Teams (Problem Resolution Circles)
On-line	Partnering: Operating & Staff Middle Management	Self-Directed Work Teams (Work Units)

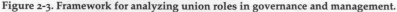

Figure 2-3. Framework for analyzing union roles in governance and management.

activity. We see the partnership providing opportunities for off-
planning, decision making, and problem solving, as well as on-line control of day-to-day operations. Furthermore, it is important to distinguish
between the institutional arrangements involving the local union leadership and those organized around the work force involved in shop floor
production. Although we have seen other U.S. joint labor-management
governance arrangements include off-line labor-management committees and teams, as well as on-line self-directed work groups, we are
aware of no other organization that has developed such an extensive
process for on-line co-management by the union.

Only two of these subprocesses appeared in the original design by
GM and the UAW, joint labor-management committees (decision rings)
and the on-line self-directed work teams (work units). Since 1985 two
other subprocesses have been developed locally by the parties. These
include off-line problem-solving teams (problem resolution circles) and
co-management through individual one-on-one partnering between the
union and management in both staff and line organizations. This last
arrangement, co-management, makes Saturn and the UAW unique in
U.S. industrial relations and directly challenges long-held assumptions
regarding the limits of labor's role in the management process.

The one-on-one partnerships were put in place throughout the management organization in the initial years before the start of production.
Individual partnerships were initiated by the local union leaders when
they recognized that they could not fulfill their managerial responsibilities as full partners simply through off-line decision rings that met
weekly. Although the SAC, MAC, and business unit decision rings provide the union opportunities for input through consensus decision making, the co-management processes of one-on-one partnering have
become more important venues for on-line influence and decision making. The development of one-on-one partnering allowed union leaders
to contribute to day-to-day management, making operating decisions
and supporting the work units.

For example, union leaders have been partnered with non-represented Saturn management through a joint selection process to carry out
new roles as operations middle management, replacing the foremen,
general foremen, and superintendents found in traditional GM plants.
Saturn's self-directed work teams are organized into modules based on
product, process, or geography. Each module has two advisors (managers) to provide guidance and resources. Although the advisors are

jointly selected by the union and Saturn management, one is represented by the UAW, and the other is not.

The union views the UAW members selected to serve in these co-management roles as supplementing the local union's elected leadership. Both partners approve payroll, overtime, and purchase orders. They also facilitate decision making with the elected team leaders. Module advisors have no authority to discharge, hire, or discipline workers. Furthermore, they do not function as stewards or committeemen because they cannot write grievances. They focus on organizing and managing resources within the team and from other support services (e.g., maintenance, engineering). Module advisors also represent their work units at the business unit labor-management committee meetings. All non-represented module advisors have union partners.

It should be noted, however, that this partnering arrangement in the production areas has not raised the indirect staffing headcount when compared with traditional plants, because each pair of module advisors is responsible for supporting an average of one hundred production employees. This high direct-to-indirect ratio of approximately 50 to 1 results from both the unique role of the module advisor and the design of the work teams, which are empowered to assume many of the responsibilities of traditional foremen. In most GM plants, direct-to-indirect staffing in production areas averages 25 to 1.[11] Even NUMMI, with its team-based, lean production system, operates at a direct-to-indirect ratio of 18 to 1.[12]

Each business unit also has partnered crew coordinators who are organized across each shift and are responsible for providing leadership and resources to the module advisors and representation to the membership.

Represented module advisors were first jointly selected in 1988, and crew coordinators were added in 1989. In 1994, in response to rank-and-file calls for more forceful representation of their individual interests and needs, represented crew coordinators became elected positions and changed their role to one that is similar to grievance committee representatives in more traditional unionized plants.

From 1989 to 1990, partnering in the functional staff areas was extended to Sales, Service and Marketing; Finance; Industrial Engineering; Quality Assurance; Health and Safety; Training; Organizational Development; and Corporate Communications. Maintenance was added in 1991, and Product and Process Development in 1992.

Partnering eventually grew to include more than 400 union members, including 91 module advisors, 24 crew coordinators, 51 functional coordinators with sitewide responsibility, 53 functional coordinators at the business unit level, and 155 with module support responsibilities for quality, engineering, materials, and so forth. At various times, elected union executive board members and the four vice presidents have been partnered with business unit leaders (plant managers) or have had partnership arrangements in staff or line positions. Jointly selected union members fill the balance of the partnerships. These union partners have had the opportunity to join directly in the managerial debates and decisions that shaped Saturn's strategy. Essentially, at Saturn what would be considered middle management in most organizations contains a significant number of one-on-one partnerships between non-represented managers and their represented UAW counterparts.

Saturn is the only organization we are aware of in the United States in which union members are filling so many managerial operating and staff positions. We believe this example of labor's on-line role in management (co-management) represents the most far-reaching innovation in the Saturn governance system.

The Organization in Action: The Start-Up Years

How did this organization take shape? Recall that the Memorandum of Agreement was signed in 1985, and the choice of Spring Hill as the location for the manufacturing complex was announced in 1986. The first car did not roll off the assembly line until 1990. The first five years of Saturn's life were taken up in building the organization before it built cars. A brief review of how the partnership contributed to building the organization during these formative years helps to set the stage for understanding what was to come later. The joint processes envisioned for the organization began with the initial tasks of product development and selection of component suppliers. Following are some examples of critical union input into key decisions in these areas. We have also included similar examples for marketing, planning, employee selection, training, and development.

Product Development

The union had significant impact on product development in the Powertrain plant (engine and transmission production and assembly), in its decisions about lost foam casting of components. UAW team members argued for building prototypes on the same fixtures that were to be used in production, a recommendation not originally supported by engineering. In implementing this recommendation, the team members found they could not perform the assembly on the intended fixtures and had to modify them. Thus, Saturn was able to simultaneously debug both the product and the assembly process, which convinced management of the benefit of early involvement of union members in product and process design.

In 1989 and 1990 Saturn engaged in a great deal of internal discussion about how to expand its product line. Saturn's marketing organization and retailers wanted a convertible and a station wagon. Both could not be introduced at the same time, and the convertible had structural problems that needed to be solved. The local union supported the position of introducing the station wagon first, arguing that although the convertible carried more product image for Saturn, the station wagon represented higher potential sales and therefore improved employment security. A consensus was reached to introduce the station wagon first. Similarly, the original plan called for Saturn to build a hatchback, but input from the retailer representatives convinced planners that a coupe would sell better. So, again, the participation of these stakeholders influenced the strategic choices involving the product portfolio in a manner unprecedented in GM's history.

Union involvement in the product development process continued in later years, as modifications to the original models and expansions in the product offerings were brought on line. The union (along with engineering) assisted in the 1999 record launch of the highly successful three-door coupe. The local union, however, experienced more difficulty in gaining support for a set of second-generation products, even though it pushed GM throughout the mid-1990s for new products and additional plant capacity. These debates culminated in the 1998 negotiations in which GM first promised to study and later committed to building a SUV in Spring Hill.

Suppliers

The union was a full partner in supplier selection and helped to develop a sourcing process from 1986 to 1989. The original 1985 Memorandum of Agreement states that "Consistent with being quality and cost competitive, a goal of Saturn is to utilize American-made components in assembly of its vehicles."[13]

The union appointed representatives to each of more than 300 product development teams that brought together product engineers, manufacturing engineers, material managers, and financial/accounting managers. These teams qualified suppliers on the basis of a formula that evaluated quality, costs, delivery, reliability, and labor relations. They reached consensus recommendations that were forwarded to the UAW International and Saturn management for review and approval.

Both management and the union reported a great deal of early struggle in supplier selection. Only over time were common goals established for quality and price. The UAW International maintained a strong preference for GM-allied suppliers employing UAW members. Non-allied UAW shops were seen as the next best choice, followed by non-allied union shops. If GM-allied suppliers were not chosen, the UAW International would often put a hold on the decision. Partnerships were then established between Saturn and allied as well as non-allied UAW suppliers to help them qualify. Help would include the development of a plan and demonstration of commitment to improve quality and productivity. For example, when the initial decision for a supplier of headlamps was heading toward a Japanese firm, the UAW International helped the GM Inland Fisher Guide division qualify as the supplier through an agreement to have them acquire the Japanese technology to produce the headlamps domestically. Thus, the UAW took on the role of upgrading the quality and operations of its member firms to help them qualify as suppliers while maintaining the integrity of Saturn's standards.

The result was development of a supplier network that provided 90 percent U.S. and more than 95 percent North American content. Over the years, the local union continued to be active in new supplier selection and in some cases has acted to defend Saturn's decisions from GM and UAW International pressure to choose GM suppliers.

Marketing and Retailer Relationships

The union also participates directly in the selection of retailers (note the use of the term "retailers," not "dealers"). Saturn envisioned and implemented a new and unique distribution and sales structure and philosophy for attracting and retaining customers. Although we have not studied the retail side of the organization, we are fortunate that several colleagues from MIT's International Motor Vehicle Program have done so. They found many of the same partnership principles at work in Saturn's relationship to its retailers:

Several inferences have already been made in this [working] paper to the importance of partnership between Saturn and its retailers. In order to achieve higher customer satisfaction, Saturn has ceded substantial power to its retailers: the larger territories make Saturn more dependent on each retailer, and Saturn has committed to include retailers in its own internal decision-making process. The retailers in return are also more dependent on the manufacturer, as they have to make larger investments and make larger commitments to corporate standards. For example, Saturn retailers must invest $2 to $3 million in their facility, and they legally commit to not "dual" (in the same store) other manufacturers' brands. This type of control exchange is often referred to as an exchange of hostages in the institutional economics literature. . . .

However, the Saturn partnership is more than checks and balances of power. It is based on Saturn's philosophy of empowering all stakeholders in the decision making of the firm. This partnership is the basis for a common vision between manufacturer and retailer so that they are working together toward common goals.[14]

As the quotation indicates, Saturn would sell cars through Saturn retail stores that could carry no other brands. Prices were fixed and non-negotiable, so customers would not worry about getting a bad deal. The sales process was customer focused, with little pressure and an emphasis on service and education. Saturn retailers invested heavily in training, including sending employees to Spring Hill. Customer satisfaction became the highest priority in the hope of building a loyal customer base that would repeat purchase and enthusiastically recommend Saturn to their friends and family. Customer service representatives were included in the retail operation to ensure satisfaction with both the sales and service experience. The Customer Action Council (CAC) was established in parallel to the partnership structures that guided the labor-management relationship. It consisted of representatives of the retailers along with management and union representatives. And, as any Saturn owner knows, the UAW partner to the manager in charge of marketing at Saturn co-signs all of the correspondence customers receive as a normal part of the follow-up to their sales and service visits to a Saturn retailer.

The union was involved in the development of the new customer-focused sales approaches, which included non-negotiable pricing; it participated in the selection of the corporate advertising agency; and it was an early supporter of the highly publicized 1991 decision to replace rather than repair cars containing a defective coolant.

This approach to marketing, sales, and service was quite a change from the traditional GM management culture and, not surprisingly, met with some initial skepticism and resistance. For example, when union representatives began their discussions with, and selection of, potential retailers, Saturn's marketing and sales officials resisted the UAW's involvement in the process. This resistance slowly subsided over time, as union representatives demonstrated their ability to help convince potential retailers to invest in what was once seen as a risky undertaking. Both management and local UAW leadership now agree that it was the union, in discussing the partnership and Saturn's commitment to quality with potential retailers, that had the greatest influence in convincing them to individually invest the necessary $3 million. According to Skip LeFauve, Saturn president from 1986 to 1996, "In order for partnership and [the] consensus decision-making process to have meaning, each party must put something at risk. The significance of UAW involvement in retailer selection is the commitment made to quality. They put themselves at risk, on the line for performance."

Over the years, the UAW has been integral in decisions affecting both retailers and customers. The UAW found ways to assist the retailers through floor plan assistance, leases, and reward programs. It helped institute cost reductions in the fall of 1997 (pushing for $750 instead of the $500 recommended by marketing) and insisted that recent customers be given rebates. The union also successfully pushed for the use of fleet sales, something Saturn had resisted for many years. In addition, the union developed the Union Marketing Initiative, in which it works with retailers to develop relationships with unions in their geographic areas. In addition to car sales to union members (without discounts), union members build playgrounds, fund scholarships, and coordinate blood drives and organ donation together. Saturn has provided $1 million in funding.

Union representatives participate on the Franchise Operating Team decision ring as well as the CAC. In these arenas, the UAW has created alliances with retailers, sometimes differing with executives who tend to give greater weight to the effects of a decision on the corporation's short-term bottom line.

Partnership Planning

The local union leadership developed annual Partnership Implementation Plans each year from 1986 through 1990. These plans served to interpret and expand the initial 1985 Memorandum of Agreement and outlined detailed steps for the union's development, implementation, and administration of the partnership throughout Saturn. It is out of these plans that the partnering in middle management evolved.

Work Force Selection

Saturn's first wave of hiring, from November 1986 to October 1991, brought on the first crew. Those hired during this period voluntarily left jobs in other GM facilities to come to Saturn. During this period, union members were required to give up their rights to transfer back to GM, whereas managers were not. Over time, however, as GM downsized and closed plants during the late 1980s and early 1990s, an agreement was made with the UAW International to recruit only from the pool of employees who were currently or scheduled to be laid off. The second wave of hiring, from 1992 to 1993, included mostly younger workers who had been laid off from GM with no recall rights. Saturn sent out approximately 17,000 letters to recruit these people, many of whom had been laid off for several years. These people filled the second and third crews. Hiring continued to accelerate the production schedule and fill openings created by retirements. The last wave of hiring followed the 1993 GM negotiations in which 21 plant closings were announced. From January 1994 to 1996, jobs were offered only to people whose plants closed or were slated to close. These were high-seniority people, often with fifteen, twenty, or more years at GM. In February 1996 after these individuals were offered opportunities, Saturn offered the last three hundred positions to local people from Tennessee. Those hired in the early years, who voluntarily left GM jobs to come to Saturn, and those who came to Saturn because they had been laid off or their plants were closing had different attitudes toward the Saturn partnership.

The recruitment and selection process was jointly developed and administered through a battery of tests conducted over a week's time. To be offered a job by Saturn, the team in which an individual would ultimately work would have to make a recommendation to hire. Skills and abilities, not seniority, were the basis for selection.

Training and Development

New Saturn members received from 350 to 700 hours of training before they were allowed to build the car. The work force is trained in work team organization, problem solving, decision making, conflict resolution, and labor history. Furthermore, they develop skills in areas traditionally reserved for management, including budgeting, business planning and scheduling, cost analysis, manufacturing methods, ergonomics, industrial engineering, job design, accounting, record keeping, statistical process control, design of experiments, and data analysis. Recognizing the need for a highly skilled work force, the union proposed linking the implementation of organizationwide training to the risk-and-reward compensation plan (discussed in greater detail below). The result was a requirement that every Saturn employee receive an additional 92 hours of training each year. This commitment to education is unique among manufacturing organizations. Because all employees receive the same high level of training, however, it is difficult to assess the impact of this investment on the partnership organization.

Two Conflicting Views of Early Saturn

Around 1990, after production was begun and five years after the signing of the initial Memorandum of Agreement, visitors to Saturn would have seen an organization that was truly a "different kind of company." Whether one was excited and optimistic about what one saw depended on one's expectation for what a company should look like and the goals it should aspire to achieve. Consider two different points of view from MIT colleagues who visited Saturn in these early years. One view was summarized in the notes of Robert McKersie, who spent considerable time at Saturn between 1985 and 1990. He brings an industrial relations perspective and an eye that is sensitive to the way different interests are articulated and how difficult issues are surfaced and resolved:

> Over the summer (1990), I spent ten days sitting in on meetings of the Strategic Action Council, the Manufacturing Action Council, various business unit meetings, the Resources Quality Council, the Customer Action Council/Franchise Operating Team and the Operating Team in the Body Calibration Department.
>
> General Observations
>
> 1. Given the ingredients of Saturn: a new car design, new location, and [at that time] 3,000 employees drawn from all over the country, I believe that the organizational design that has been selected was

absolutely critical. With so many new items, the only way to accomplish all of the required learning is with a highly involved and motivated organization. The organization design that includes partnership, consensus and teams achieves this required high level of commitment. . .

2. The partnership process is impressive. First, UAW representatives play key roles at all levels of the organization, and I have seen their presence in council meetings as the major "truth serum." [For example] it is clear that the role of the UAW partners is absolutely pivotal for the functioning of Saturn. At the most recent meeting of the SAC, the only individuals who were willing to take issue and to "tell it like it is" were the UAW representatives. Other participants in the meeting did not speak their minds as freely and tended to back off when the CEO expressed a point of view. . .

3. The partnership that is developing with dealers is especially impressive . . . I attended a two-day meeting of CAC and saw the dealers in action. Several of the dealers remarked to me that they had gone through a "religious experience" as a result of the Saturn partnership and they could not abide any longer their arm's length relationships with other car companies.

4. Based on one intense meeting in the Powertrain business unit, I would conclude that the integration of design and manufacturing is working well. At this meeting, key members of the engineering organization met with key members of the manufacturing organization and worked through a very complicated agenda . . .

5. I attended [a] meeting of an operating team . . . this team conducted what I thought was one of the best meetings that I have attended. In fact, decision rings lower in the organization appear to operate more effectively than those at the top of the organization . . .

In contrast, consider the impressions our colleague Dan Roos had on his first visit to Saturn when he accompanied a team of us in early 1991, shortly after the start of production. Roos, the director of MIT's International Motor Vehicle Program, had just published the best-selling book from that project, *The Machine that Changed the World*, in which he and his coauthors argued for the virtues of lean production.[15] Lean production is focused solely on achieving the highest levels of productivity and quality with use of what are essentially the Toyota production methods and design principles. Viewing Saturn through the lens of lean production, Roos was troubled by what he saw and concerned that Saturn would fail. It was not lean production. Consensus decision making meant compromises and delays. By bringing the UAW into the management process, the singular focus of lean production would be lost. He also feared Saturn was trying to do too many new things at once—introduce new technology (e.g., lost foam casting, plastic body panels, movable pallets on the assembly line), a new vehicle, single-source suppliers, and a new distribution strategy, as well as the new labor-management partnership and manufacturing system.

In some ways, both interpretations were accurate. Saturn does not use all the features of lean production, although it uses many of the features of the lean production model. Instead, Saturn was designed to include the union in firm management and governance and serve multiple objectives of multiple stakeholders—GM shareholders were to get a specific product, a small car, that would be profitable but that would also recapture sales in this market segment lost to Japanese competitors in the first half of the 1980s. GM employees would get jobs with a high degree of participation and control, jobs that otherwise would have been located in overseas firms that could produce the small cars GM needed for growth. American supplier firms and their employees would likewise get new business and job opportunities. A new set of retailers would similarly have new business opportunities. And all these parties would have a learning laboratory designed in risky and innovative ways from which they could learn and adapt their existing organizations or pattern new operations.

Saturn as a Stakeholder Firm and Networked Organization

Instead of imitating lean production, Saturn embodied what we have come to call a stakeholder firm and networked organization.[16] Saturn was set up to achieve multiple objectives of multiple parties rather than to simply conform to the single goal of the American firm that seeks to maximize shareholder value. Thus, lean production principles are important to build cars competitively, but so are the number of jobs created, employment standards (e.g., wage and benefit levels, working conditions), and employment security. Employees shared in the risks and potential rewards of the enterprise both through the compensation formula and the lack of equivalent alternatives (giving up seniority and transfer rights back to GM) if Saturn failed. Thus, employees became, in the technical terms, "residual risk bearers"—they risked their human capital in the same way GM investors and retailers and suppliers risked their financial capital. In return, employees and their union would participate directly in the governance of the firm, and human resource practices were designed to achieve high levels of commitment, effort, and performance from knowledge workers through all levels of the work force. Given these stakeholder objectives and goals, the performance of Saturn must ultimately be judged not narrowly, and solely in terms of its profitability and return to shareholders, but also against the multiple concerns and objectives of these different stakeholders.

This, in our view, is the most radical of all the implications of what emerged from the risks that the original champions for innovation within GM and the UAW took in creating the Committee of 99 to explore how they could work together and meet their shared and separate interests. But was the American business community, let alone future leaders of GM and the UAW, ready to accept these same principles? This was not something the initial visionaries thought much about at the time. In retrospect, it is unfortunate that they didn't foresee how radical and controversial an organization they were about to create. If they had, they most likely would have taken steps to ensure that support for it would live on after they left the organization.

Conclusion

In the initial design and start-up Saturn truly was a "different kind of company," with all the attendant risks, potential rewards, and uncertainty and controversy associated with breaking so many traditions and norms of past business, organization, and labor-management practice. But, could this organization build cars?

One might conclude from this brief history of the innovations that led up to Saturn that Saturn embodies the basic principles that Reuther articulated for the labor movement in the 1940s but failed to achieve in the face of strong opposition of the business leaders and his fellow union leaders. The partnership and co-management structures in some ways also represent the pinnacle of the transformation of the traditional industrial relations system that began with tentative experiments with QWL; moved on to team work systems; and then, at Saturn, moved to participation throughout the organization, from the shop floor, to co-management, to the highest levels of strategic managerial decision making. This is the positive spin on the architecture of Saturn.

In spite of this positive spin, however, there were strong critics within both union and management circles. Victor Reuther, Walter's surviving brother, for example, would blast Saturn for giving up many of the hard-fought bargaining provisions on seniority and for embracing a form of enterprise unionism he and Walter fought to overcome in the formative and glory years of the UAW. Within management, critics were equally vociferous, arguing that GM gave away its ability to manage—something GM in particular had staunchly protected in bargaining since Wilson rejected Walter Reuther's arguments in the 1940s.

These are highly rhetorical and ideologically charged arguments. They cannot be resolved in the abstract. We need to look at the actual experience at Saturn.

3

The Partnership in Action

aturn's mission is "to market vehicles developed and manufactured
in the United States that are world leaders in quality, cost, and customer satisfaction through the integration of people, technology
and business systems." How well has it done in implementing the different dimensions of this mission? We explore this question in this chapter
by examining the Saturn partnership in action. Because we believe the
real lessons from Saturn lie in its teams and co-management processes,
we give considerable emphasis to these internal aspects of its operations.
Before turning to these features, however, we summarize how Saturn
performed on some of the key measurements relevant to its mission.

Performance Measurements

We begin with performance measures of interest to the work force and
the UAW. In terms of retaining jobs that had otherwise been moving overseas, Saturn clearly has made a major contribution. Approximately 8,300
UAW bargaining unit jobs were created, including the new amalgamated
units organized by the local union. This number remained steady through
1999. For most of the years, Saturn workers' wages (net of overtime, for
which no comparison data are available) exceeded those of their General
Motors counterparts. Saturn's wages have been pegged to a percentage of
GM's (varying from 88 percent to 95 percent, depending on when they
were negotiated). The risk portion of risk-and-reward (i.e., the amount
below the GM rate) is satisfied by achieving the target of ninety-two hours

per year of training for each employee. By achieving these targets, employees brought their wages up equal to the GM level. The reward portions of wages above this level are contingent on meeting mutually negotiated goals for quality, cost, schedule, profitability, and volume. The reward bonus history has been $2,600 in 1992, $3,000 in 1993, $6,400 in 1994, $10,000 in 1995, $10,000 in 1996, $2,017 in 1997, $3,300 in 1998, and $6,200 in 1999. By comparison, in addition to their base compensation, GM employees are eligible for a profit-sharing bonus that has averaged $500 during this period. Thus, without accounting for overtime earnings, Saturn employees have earned more than their GM counterparts.

Saturn has done very well in meeting its objectives for quality and customer satisfaction. The best data on this come from the industry standard, J. D. Power and Associates. Their customer satisfaction index showed that in 1992, after only two years of production, and every year since, Saturn has led domestic car lines in consumer ratings based on vehicle quality, reliability, and satisfaction after one year of ownership. Saturn's rating each year has also exceeded all brands worldwide, with the exception of Lexus and Infiniti (Acura and Mercedes in 1997 only), which are much costlier luxury lines.[1]

Productivity, costs, and profitability have proven to be more variable. The variability in Saturn's productivity performance, as tracked by the industrywide Harbour and Associates benchmarking data, illustrates this point. In 1994 and 1995, Saturn's assembly plant productivity ranked either first or second among all GM plants (although still well below the best in the industry). These performance levels were achieved even though the original production levels that were planned for Saturn (500,000 units per year) had been cut back nearly 40 percent by GM corporate decision makers. So, three to four years after the start-up of production, Saturn was doing reasonably well on this performance metric. By 1997 and 1998, however, Saturn had fallen considerably, in absolute levels of productivity (as measured in labor hours per vehicle) and relative to other GM plants. Its 1998 numbers came in just slightly below GM's overall average. As Harbour and Associates indicated, some of this was inevitable, given the no-layoff commitment at Saturn. For example, in 1998, instead of laying off workers Saturn absorbed the equivalent of sixteen days without production by having workers engage in training and perform a range of other work and community service activities.[2] Thus, although at its peak Saturn's productivity was as good or better than any other GM facility, it never reached the levels of the best plants in the United States or Japan that implemented a full lean production model. As a stakeholder-based organization, it may not be expected to do so in the same way, because by design it seeks to balance multiple operational objectives regarding productivity, costs, quality, customer image, and job security. But clearly, Saturn was set up to achieve productivity and quality levels well above those obtainable in the traditional GM-UAW plants. Operating at full capacity, it appeared to do so. Although some of its more recent productivity decline is clearly due to the softening of the small-car market and its own sales decline as its original model aged, some is also a reflection of an inadequate process for continuous improvement.

Saturn did set the benchmark for GM (and perhaps for other automakers as well) in its launch performance of new products in 1996, 1997, 1998, and again in 1999. The key performance metrics for judging the success of a new product launch are the number of units of production sacrificed during the retooling and ramp-up period, the number of days production is shut down completely, and the number of days required to get back up to full production levels. In each of these years, Saturn's launch performance set the standard for GM. Typically, GM takes anywhere from 60 to more than 300 days to get back to prelaunch production levels, and the opportunity cost of lower production levels is significant. In the launch of the 1996 sedan, for example, it took Saturn only 30 days to get back to the prelaunch level of the 1995 car while continuing to maintain quality. Saturn experienced no lost production in the 1997 launch, and in 1999, when it introduced the new three-door coupe and made substantial changes to its sedan and station wagon models, it did so without losing any days due to the changeover and accelerated to full production in 22 days, losing only 2,300 vehicles to the ramp-up process. Saturn's launch performance has gained widespread recognition in GM.

Saturn's profitability is difficult to judge, because there is no clear consensus regarding how much of the up-front costs for starting the new division and developing Saturn's initial models should be charged against the division or the overall corporation, and there have been ongoing debates over whether Saturn could be expected to be profitable at the authorized annual volume level of 330,000 vehicles rather than the 500,000 on which the original business plan was built. Saturn turned its first operating profits in 1993, after being pressured by GM to break even two years ahead of the original plan. In 1995 and 1996, internal company documents showed that Saturn produced higher profits per vehicle than any other units in GM's small-car division. But when sales of all small cars, including Saturns, declined in the period from 1997 to 1999, so too did these profit margins. Again, as with the productivity data, Saturn's profits are more sensitive to these declines than other parts of GM, because the work force could be reduced only through attrition.

Taking these different dimensions into consideration, one could view Saturn's performance as a glass half-full or half-empty, depending on the specific metric and time period on which one focuses. The half-full view would note that when supported by fresh products and a strong market, the Saturn system outperformed its GM counterparts on most, if not all, of the critical metrics—quality, productivity, profitability, new product launch, wages, and job security. And it did so with former GM workers, some of whom volunteered for Saturn and some who came to work there only because they had no other alternative at GM. The half-empty view, on the other hand, would note that the productivity and profitability metrics eroded on both an absolute and relative scale as Saturn encountered difficulties in its markets. What these data suggest is that there is both considerable upside potential and downside risk to the Saturn model. There is no natural or automatic performance advantage, and no liability is associated with it—the results depend on how the model is implemented and managed. Therefore, we need to look at to the inner workings of Saturn over these years.

Inner Workings

The Saturn partnership structure evolved to include the four distinct dimensions or subprocesses introduced in Figure 2-3 of Chapter 2: (1) on-line self-directed work teams, (2) off-line problem-solving groups, (3) joint labor-management committees, or decision rings, as they are called at Saturn, and (4) the co-management partnering arrangements found throughout the management structure. In the remainder of this chapter, we review how these features of the partnership evolved and operated in practice, focusing on how the parties gave life to the vision embodied in the original Saturn agreement and then slowly created and reinforced a culture of co-management unique in the annals of American business and labor relations history. Yet, the legacy of Saturn's parents—GM and the UAW—will also be visible in this account, because the managers and union leaders at Saturn were only partly successful in shedding old habits and customs.

Work Teams and Modules

The team-based work units at Saturn are the basic building blocks of the organization, both in design and in practice. The Memorandum of Agreement states, for example, the following:

The structure of Saturn reflects certain basic principles, e.g., placement of authority and decision making in the most appropriate part of the organization, with emphasis on the Work Unit (p. 4).

The time we spent at Saturn has convinced us that these team-based work units, and the modules into which related teams are grouped, are in fact the foundation on which Saturn's successes and, when it has fallen on hard times, its failures rest. Members of the teams are extremely well trained, have significant control over the quality and pace of their work, and hold the knowledge needed to produce the high quality and retain the customer satisfaction to which Saturn is dedicated. We have seen that, when highly motivated and given the resources, support, and leadership, Saturn teams solve problems and achieve production, new product launches, and quality targets equivalent to world-class benchmarks.

During, an interview we conducted in the Panel Assembly module, a team leader came into the office saying that a team member thought the torque on his drill was improper for tightening down the panel under the wiper blades. Improper torque would lead to a loose panel and possibly some rattling. The module advisor called ahead to the Car Final module and asked his counterpart there to check the wiper panels, which turned out to be loose. Furthermore, cars with loose panels had already left the plant and were being loaded in rail cars and trucks for shipping. If a similar problem occurred at a GM plant, upper management would be contacted for a decision regarding whether to repair the defect on site or leave it to the dealers. At Saturn, the module advisor approached the representative of the company that ships the finished vehicles and assumes liability for the cars once they leave Car Final. The representative stated that Saturn employees could no longer have access to the vehicles. Rather than leave the repair to the dealers or wait for a decision at higher levels, the module advisor from Panels, the team leader, and team quality-point person ignored the shipping company representative and went outside to the cars waiting to be shipped. In the line of vehicles waiting to be shipped, they found the first vehicle with a loose panel and worked their way back to the plant, hand-tightening all defects. This rapid response was unusual, as was the willingness to take risks and responsibility for fixing problems rather than send them up the chain of command for a decision, as would be the case in more traditional GM plants. The behavior indicated a high level of organizational commitment and strong horizontal communication and coordination.

In another example, when Saturn set the benchmark within GM for its performance in launching new products between 1996 and 1999, it did so with what it called its "build-bucket" approach, a technique developed and first used in 1996. In preparation for production of the 1996 sedan, work units (teams) were given build buckets containing the components for the new vehicle. In the months before the July 1995 launch, they were asked to analyze manufacturing or assembly problems caused by the shift to the new parts and design. Module advisors then surveyed every work unit, accumulated the problems, and categorized them. Issues were then assigned to problem-solving teams made up of engineers, work unit members, and suppliers. The same approach was repeated even more successfully in the launch of the 1997 coupe. Since the risk-and-reward formula included production schedule targets, the launch performance resulted in Saturn team members receiving $10,000 bonuses for both 1995 and 1996 (the reward was capped at that level). This experience, like many others, illustrates the extraordinary capacity of Saturn's partnership organization to pull together and coordinate problem-solving efforts. Saturn's teams can and do solve many problems that are within their control.

When problems in the larger organization demotivate team members, however, the effects on productivity can be quite negative, as the Harbour data reported earlier showed for 1997 and 1998. The building blocks are strong, but their performance depends on what happens in the larger organizational setting.

Not all of Saturn's productivity decline should be attributed to its no-layoff policy. There is no question in our minds that some of the decline is also due to the declining morale and trust we observed and to a weakening of the partnership at Saturn in recent years. For example, the softening of the small-car market in 1997 and 1998 increased tension between the local union and GM around the lack of new products for Saturn. It also created, for the first time, job insecurity among Saturn employees. Bonuses based on production were reduced, and negotiations were conducted early in 1998 to revise the risk-and-reward formula. Several months later, while a number of other locals were striking GM, UAW

Local 1853 (at Saturn) voted for strike authorization, giving their leaders thirty days to settle disagreements with the company. The resulting negotiations focused on resources for new products, the risk-and-reward formula, and decision-making authority (see Chapter 4 for more discussion of these events). Although quality performance continued to show steady improvement throughout this time, setting a new record for GM corporate audits, manufacturing and assembly hours per vehicle rose during both crisis periods. Interviews with Saturn team members, module advisors, and crew coordinators during January 1999 provide some interesting insights on behaviors and attitudes during this difficult year:

Represented Crew Coordinator

This summer was very frustrating for a crew coordinator when you can't provide answers to the floor. I just didn't have anything. The negotiators were told not to talk to us because they didn't want rumors and leaks. So, we went for like a month with nothing, but yet we told them the best thing we could do is keep building a quality car and keep moving production. Are they going to pay us our money, are we gonna be laid off, is this going to happen, is that going to happen? Let's just keep building quality cars. Whatever comes out of that we just hope for the best and they [the teams] kept going. It was amazing.

Non-Represented Module Advisor

We have the same amazing quality we had back then. The quality numbers are pretty much the same, they stayed consistent. As far as running the line, there was never any sort of a situation where a line wasn't going to run. I never felt like tomorrow they're not going to work. That's different I think at Saturn than it is maybe at GM . . . So to me coming in here and knowing that I can count on these guys to run the line and get the quality, even through all the times we went through last year. These guys were there for me, and we're still running and doing the right thing. That's a good feeling for a module advisor. So, I was very proud to be a part of Saturn last year.

Represented Module Advisor

They got a 5.7 [an excellent score on GM's internal quality audit metric]. That's unheard of in the company. I saw the morale just kick right up on into the third and fourth quarter where I've never seen it before.

Team Member

There was a time where the sales were sort of down in the middle of last year, and a lot of people around me, on my team in my area, they were

dwelling on "if we continue to make this car at perfection and keep getting quality and awards for doing such a great job, this is what's going to
keep us hauling them in the market so we won't get totally wiped out."
We had to try to dwell on the Saturn nameplate as one that's quality
building to keep the customers saying "I could get a Chevy but [with] a
Saturn I'll be worry free, no problem, no hassle on down the line," and
that's what kicked in as far as you see as far as the [quality audit] scores.
Nobody really ever lost the zeal of doing a quality job, even during all
the things that was going on.

These comments reinforce what we have consistently observed in our
visits to Spring Hill. Saturn's frontline teams and, more specifically, their
team members are the key asset and source of competitive advantage to
the company.

Off-Line Problem-Solving Groups

As powerful as the teams are, we noted as early as 1992 that Saturn
was having difficulty making off-line problem-solving work effectively.
Off-line problem-solving teams are particularly important for taking up
issues that exceed the scope of authority, resources, or tasks residing
within specific work teams. Coordination with engineering, maintenance, or suggestions that require approval of higher management levels, or issues that require investigation or cut across teams all require
off-line problem solving. In some organizations, particularly at Honda
and Toyota, management has traditionally used off-line problem solving
to focus on specific problems of high priority. One year (or month) safety
might be chosen as the focus because the number of incidents has risen.
Another time, costs or warranty problems might become the target for
continuous improvement. Supervisors are expected to focus on generat-
ing suggestions for addressing these priorities.

At Saturn, on the other hand, regular off-line problem solving had not
received high priority. Instead, resources were focused on the on-line, self-
directed work teams that were expected to solve problems within their
unit informally on a daily basis and to focus on controlling and standard-
izing their processes. Although this type of problem solving is important,
as Japanese auto producers have demonstrated, it is not a substitute for
rigorous off-line, continuous efforts directed at solving broader product or
process problems. Off-line problem solving typically requires patient and
systematic research and analysis over time to pursue root-cause solutions

with teams that combine employees with a variety of skills and functional expertise from across different parts of the organization.

As experiences from the 1996 and 1997 launch illustrate, Saturn has demonstrated that it can pull together problem-solving groups on an exception basis to address specific problems. In 1992 GM put pressure on all its units, including Saturn, to help reduce its mounting losses (see Chapter 5). In response, the union led a massive problem-solving effort directed at improving Saturn's financial performance. Specifically, the local mounted an organizationwide effort to identify cost-saving opportunities, which resulted in 1,150 suggestions from team members. Follow-through from the MAC was limited, however, and that massive effort was not institutionalized. In 1993, senior management and union leaders at Saturn made an effort to create a more effective off-line problem-solving process. We worked with Saturn leaders (plant managers, MAC and SAC members, union leaders) to organize a two-day workshop during which Saturn's problem-solving efforts were benchmarked against those of Japanese- and U.S.-owned companies operating in the United States. By the end of the meeting, the MAC had agreed to follow through, but by the spring of 1999 less than 10 percent of Saturn employees were involved in ongoing off-line problem-solving teams. Lack of follow through has been an ongoing problem with leadership at Saturn.

During this same period, our interviews with team members, as well as feedback obtained from both one-on-one interviews with non-represented managers conducted by management and similar interviews conducted by the local union of its members, revealed concern with a deterioration in Saturn's organizational culture and leadership. The internal union report summarizing both represented and non-represented interviews noted,

There are many concerns about Saturn's organizational culture, and it is the #1 issue raised in the "Member-to-Member" survey by a large margin. Team members still feel that Saturn is the best company they've ever worked for and are glad to be here. They find Saturn refreshing, and many feel positive about the culture, the people philosophy, and the entrepreneurial aspects . . . However, there is deep concern that Saturn is drifting away from our mission, philosophy, and values and headed quickly back toward the traditional GM culture we should be seeking to change.

Leadership was the #3 issue. (Compensation issues were the #2 concern.) There were some positive comments about Saturn leaders in general, noting supportiveness, proactiveness, etc. Most often cited were the need for leaders to be more decisive, to provide more direction, to

communicate better, be more cohesive, and to "walk the talk" better . . .
One of the biggest concerns is the perception that Saturn is top heavy,
with too many layers of management, and another is that leadership is
not held accountable, nor made to follow through.

These data reinforce a conclusion we reached from our own interviews and interactions at Saturn. For reasons we cannot not fully understand, an effective model of managerial leadership suitable for directing
and motivating team members did not develop or was not reinforced.
We believe this is the primary reason why an off-line problem-solving
process capable of achieving continuous improvement, as opposed to
periodic responses to specific crises or problems, did not take hold at
Saturn (historically, it has also not been a priority at GM).

Decision Rings

The joint labor-management committees at each level of the partnership—SAC (corporate), MAC (site), business unit, module, and work
unit (team)—share information and provide an opportunity for input
and decision making. In the words of one plant manager at Saturn,

> [The decision rings are] used here as more of a communication medium
> to get the word out to the floor, what's going on, what changes are com-
> ing, and what procedural changes we're making . . . When you finally
> reach a decision, it's slower, but you usually make a better decision.
> You've got everybody's buy-in. You're not trying to force your ideas all
> the way down to the floor to make it go.

These committees are very much part of the Saturn culture and a radical departure from the world of GM, which most Saturn employees
have experienced. As one union executive board member described the
difference,

> The biggest difference [from GM] I found is that when I was at my old
> job, you [labor] were never a part of identifying problems. You were
> always out there bitching and moaning about problems, but when it
> came time to get into a huddle in the room and resolve it, you were never
> part of that. You are never part of the conversation. Management would
> go off into one room and do their thing, and we would go off in our room
> and do our thing. We would get back together, and they would lay their
> plan in front of you and want you to buy into it. Well, it's a lot harder to
> buy into a plan you haven't been part of. Part of buying into it is concep-

tualization of an idea, looking at all the different alternatives, and once you've explored all those alternatives, no matter what you come out with, you are a lot more committed. It very well could be that they could come out with a good idea, but because you weren't part of that thought process, you didn't buy into it. You are always suspicious, "Did they think about this; did they do that?"

These groups are scheduled to meet weekly for one to several hours, with the SAC meeting Mondays, MAC Tuesdays, business units Wednesdays, modules Thursdays, and teams Fridays. This schedule was designed to encourage rapid transmission of information throughout the organization as well as the integration and implementation of key decisions made at higher levels.

During the early 1990s, the SAC met on a regular basis to discuss strategic issues, including productivity, new products, capacity utilization, retailing, suppliers, investments, and relations with GM and the international union. For example, the SAC drove the push for profitability in the first few years after Saturn began production. As early as 1992, expansion to a second Saturn plant (Mod II) was a regular topic of conversation, as was the ongoing question of how Saturn fits within GM's worldwide strategy. By 1994, SAC concerns had shifted to moves by GM to centralize decision making and integrate Saturn's products with those of other divisions.

Like the MAC, however, the SAC has often had difficulty in following through on decisions. We witnessed discussions on the need to organize a formal team-based problem-solving effort focused on continuous improvement and on the need to create a process for organizational learning, but these received limited follow-through by the SAC. Throughout the 1990s, there has been ongoing criticism of the lack of accountability for implementing decisions. During 1998 and much of 1999, the SAC was no longer meeting weekly, and by June 1999, Cynthia Trudell, Saturn's new president, attempted to reinvigorate the committee by scheduling two-day meetings every other week.

In part, the accountability problem may have its roots in the decentralization of decision making and autonomy among Saturn's three business units. Each business unit has its own culture, which can be traced to its parent organization in GM—Fisher Body for Body Systems, GM Hydromatic for Powertrain, and GM Assembly Division for Vehicle Systems. Saturn is the only entity within GM in which these three divisions come together in one organization. There is wide variation in the way the partnership has been implemented in each plant, as will seen in our survey data, reported later in this chapter. Furthermore, turnover has been high among the plant managers/business team leaders. In 1993, we found the average tenure to be less than one year, and the same situation continued to exist in 1999. Top managers see their careers tied to GM, and their decisions may include concerns about their next assignment, not simply the needs of Saturn. There is evidence that some of these managers did not invest the time and energy required to understand and become part of the Saturn culture, including developing a working partnership with their represented counterparts and reaching decisions through a consensus process within their business unit decision rings.

Co-Management

When people visit Saturn and attend formal presentations on the partnership, the on-line co-management process involving one-on-one partnering is hardly mentioned. Saturn members themselves tend to focus on the formal contractual arrangements. In fact, it was only after we spent considerable time on site that we began to see this new organizational form. Yet, it is through co-management that Saturn and the UAW have become unique in U.S. industrial relations, with institutional arrangements that directly challenge long-held assumptions regarding the limits of labor's role in the management process. Moreover, in working with Saturn, it became clear that it was through the individual one-on-one partnerships and the continuous representation of union partners in key management forums that the organizational form took its shape over the years; through it, the union added value and contributed to substantive decision making.

The development of one-on-one partnering began in 1988 with module advisors. Although management considered these positions outside the bargaining unit, the union argued that these jobs were not supervisory in the traditional sense, so its members should fill them. After months of debate on this issue, an agreement was reached that allowed the jobs to be filled by both union and non-represented employees who would work together as partners. Rather than having one module advisor for 50 team members as originally envisioned, the parties doubled the span of responsibility with two module advisors, one represented and the other not, for every 100 members.

The one-on-one partnering provides union leaders an opportunity to contribute to day-to-day management decisions and support the work units. Mike Bennett, the first president of UAW Local 1853, explained the justification he saw for having union members fill managerial positions:

> We want the voice of the worker involved in all aspects of the business. Partnership to me means, in effect, having that voice of the worker integrated into those decision-making arenas . . . One of the things [we are] attempting to do is in fact institutionalize some of those things in a systematic way. [We] are making sure there is a gatekeeper in that [decision-making] process from the workers' standpoint. . . . We established, even though the Memo [Memorandum of Agreement] didn't provide for it—it does now—a partnership here with regard to the module advisors; [these partners] will represent the interests of the module at the business team level.

Through a joint selection process, union leaders have been partnered with non-represented Saturn employees to carry out new roles as operations middle management, replacing the foremen, general foremen, and superintendents found in traditional GM plants. Joint selection operates through an interview process conducted by committees, including union and management leadership in each business unit. Candidates, both represented and non-represented, are interviewed by these committees, and recommendations are sent forward to the UAW MAC advisor and the vice president of Manufacturing for their approval.

Often during our visits we would see union leaders and managers having casual conversations, informal meetings, or scheduled meetings in which various production or other management issues were being discussed. In a visit in early 1999, for example, Bennett had to leave a session with us because he was due to meet with Saturn and GM engineers to discuss whether to use one or two production lines in assembly when the new SUV is put into production. He had his usual well-thought-out views on the issues involved and the relative merits of the two options, depending on the annual production volumes projected for the products involved. During the same period, John Michaud, the UAW representative for marketing and retailing, described in detail the integral role the union had played in developing strategies with management to support retailers and customers during the softening of the small-car market. And, as discussed above, the local worked closely with engineering to get the highly successful three-door coupe launched in record-breaking time. These are just a few instances of the many types of input union leaders bring to these discussions, as they have both the experience and the information needed to add value to what in traditional settings would have been a decision made by engineering and manufacturing managers and professionals.

Not only is this one-on-one partnering in the management process unique to American industry, it is also the hidden secret to how the union adds value to the management process at Saturn. Although the formal structures for participation (e.g., SAC, MAC) allow the union input through the consensus decision-making process, it is the co-management process that has allowed the local to become a full partner in business decisions. This is why we decided to look at this partnering in more depth and attempted to test for its effects on performance.

Quantitative Assessment of the Co-Management Process

There is considerable variation in the extent to which the co-management dimensions of the partnership are implemented across and within Saturn's three business units in Spring Hill. Recognizing this variation, we asked the question "Is there a systematic relationship between the degree to which the partnership is working in specific settings and performance?" We investigated this question at the module level by collecting data on first-time quality (FTQ) levels and quality improvement achieved in each module and relating the resulting performance indicators to data on the managerial behavior of module advisors (union-represented and non-represented) and the ways they functioned as partners. These data were then used to describe the various dynamics of the partnership and their effect on quality performance.[3]

We decided to focus on module advisors for several reasons. Theory suggests that supervision plays a critical role in team-based production systems, particularly through coordination and boundary management. Furthermore, the unique system at Saturn provided that these roles were filled by union as well as non-represented employees. Finally, all represented and non-represented module advisors were managing as partners, another innovation. We wanted to assess how these critical roles, union managers, and co-management affected performance. We chose three dimensions of the partnership to analyze empirically through surveys:

1. Because team-based manufacturing systems rely on frequent and effective internal horizontal communications to reach high levels of

performance, we expected higher levels of *communication and coordination* to be systematically related to higher levels of quality.

2. The second dimension, *balance*, is related to Saturn's attempt to transform traditional industrial relations. Although supervisors traditionally manage production and grievance committeemen handle people problems, at Saturn module advisors are responsible for both. No formal division of these responsibilities is made for the union and non-represented module advisors who in partnership manage each module. Therefore, by analyzing the balance for each manager between time spent managing production and time spent managing people, we can see whether Saturn truly departs from tradition and if balance is related to performance. If both union and non-represented module advisors balance their time between managing people and managing production, Saturn will in fact have departed from the traditional pattern of industrial relations. We hypothesized that those departments practicing this new industrial relations would produce higher levels of quality.

3. The third dimension, *alignment*, is a result of our participant observations of the partnership relations. In some modules, the represented and non-represented module advisors worked closely together, reaching decisions through a consensus process. In other modules, the partners spent little time discussing their decisions, priorities, and work tasks and managed their teams independently. We hypothesized that those union and non-represented partners who had the greatest level of alignment on goals, priorities, tasks, and responsibilities would also have higher levels of quality than did partners with lower levels of alignment.

During the second quarter of 1993, data on communications and coordination, balance, and partner alignment were collected with a set of three surveys that covered all represented and non-represented module advisors across all crews, including fifty-seven production and maintenance departments.

Figure 3-1 contains a graph of the communications network of the module advisors. It is partitioned into the three business units with Vehicle Systems (the largest business unit that performs the assembly) in the upper left, Body Systems in the center, and Powertrain (engine and transmission manufacturing) in the lower right. All module advisors were listed on the horizontal and vertical axes, and each shaded cell rep-

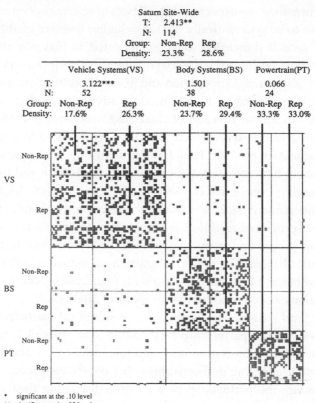

	Saturn Site-Wide	
T:	2.413**	
N:	114	
Group:	Non-Rep	Rep
Density:	23.3%	28.6%

	Vehicle Systems(VS)		Body Systems(BS)		Powertrain(PT)	
T:	3.122***		1.501		0.066	
N:	52		38		24	
Group:	Non-Rep	Rep	Non-Rep	Rep	Non-Rep	Rep
Density:	17.6%	26.3%	23.7%	29.4%	33.3%	33.0%

*   significant at the .10 level
**   significant at the .05 level
*** significant at the .01 level

Figure 3-1. Communications density among module advisors. (N = number included in survey; Nonrep = non-represented; Rep = represented; T = test of statistical significance.)

resents a communication link between two module advisors verified during the survey period.

Data for each plant is further partitioned between union and non-represented module advisors. For purposes of comparison, communications densities within each group of union and non-represented module advisors from each business unit are reported. It is interesting to note that in both Vehicle Systems and Body Systems, the mean communications densities of the union module advisors are higher than the communication densities of their non-represented counterparts. The difference in Vehicle Systems was found to be statistically significant. Powertrain densities for both groups were the same. Sitewide, the mean communications density of the union module advisors was 28.6 percent, whereas the mean communications density of the non-represented module advisors was 23.3 percent. This difference was found to be statistically significant ($p < .05$). The overall data and these comparisons suggest that the UAW module advisors have a denser network of communications than do their non-represented partners.

For purposes of comparison, we used median FTQ and FTQ improvement levels to divide Saturn's production modules into groups based on their quality performance. As we can see from the means comparison in Table 3-1, the high FTQ improvement group also had significantly greater levels of communications by the represented module advisor than did the group with low FTQ improvement. This was true for communications centrality (the overall number of communications partners) and for group centrality (communications with other represented module advisors within each plant). Most striking are the differences in communications, specifically on the subject of quality. The represented module advisors in the high quality improvement departments had almost 2.5 times the level of communications on quality than did their counterparts in the departments with low levels of quality improvement. The data showed no significant difference in overall communications centrality, group communications centrality, or quality communications between non-represented module advisors in the high quality improvement group compared with those in the low quality improvement group.

As we can see from the lower half of Table 3-1, the level of communication and coordination also appears to be related to FTQ performance. The mean overall sitewide communications centrality of the represented module advisors is significantly higher in the high FTQ group. Similarly, the mean density (the percentage of communications partners out of the total number of possible partners) of communications among represented module advisors within each plant was significantly higher in the high FTQ group. Communications on quality were significantly higher for both represented and non-represented module advisors in the high FTQ group, whereas the represented level of 3.462 for quality communications was greater than the non-represented level of 2.218. These data further illustrate the role this local union plays in the partnership by supporting higher levels of communication and coordination, which affect organizational performance.

Table 3-2 analyzes the differences between the represented and non-represented module advisors' use of time on a variety of tasks through a

Table 3-1. Comparisons of Mean Communication and Balance

Modules with High and Low Quality Improvement

	High Quality Improvement	Low Quality Improvement	T-Statistic	N
Overall Centrality				
Represented advisor	21.5	15.8	2.117**	32
	(8.13)	(6.19)		
Non-represented advisor	19.2	17.9	0.508	
	(5.13)	(4.99)		
Group Centrality				
Represented advisor	8.7	5.4	2.751**	32
	(4.02)	(2.11)		
Non-represented advisor	4.4	4.1	0.478	
	(1.45)	(1.7)		
Quality Communications				
Represented advisor	4.1	1.7	2.789**	31
	(2.08)	(1.41)		
Non-represented advisor	1.5	1.9	0.844	
	(1.32)	(1.11)		
Balance: Production and People				
Represented advisor	0.948	0.957	0.044	34
	(0.41)	(0.74)		
Non-represented advisor	1.309	2.247	2.158**	
	(0.83)	(1.62)		

Modules with High and Low First-Time Quality (FTQ)

	High FTQ	Low FTQ	T-Statistic	N
Overall Centrality				
Represented advisor	18.62	11.43	2.897***	32
	(6.98)	(5.4)		
Non-represented advisor	14.47	15	0.232	
	(6.04)	(5.79)		
Group Centrality				
Represented advisor	7.438	6.125	1.09	32
	(3.86)	(2.87)		
Non-represented advisor	4.647	3.727	1.505	
	(1.41)	(1.67)		
Group Density				
Represented advisor	0.102	0.059	4.006***	32
	(0.036)	(0.024)		
Non-represented advisor	0.091	0.104	1.025	
	(0.031)	(0.033)		
Quality Communications				
Represented advisor	3.46	1.76	2.170**	31
	(2.15)	(1.44)		
Non-represented advisor	2.21	1.12	2.603**	
	(1.13)	(1.05)		

Table 3-1. Continued

Modules with High and Low First-Time Quality (FTQ)

	High FTQ	Low FTQ	T-Statistic	N
Balance: Production and People				
Represented advisor	1.171	0.736	2.121**	34
	(0.73)	(0.42)		
Non-represented advisor	1.734	1.987	0.495	
	(1.24)	(1.62)		

*Significant at the .10 level. (Standard deviations in parentheses.)
**Significant at the .05 level.
***Significant at the .01 level.

comparison of means. Two findings are of particular importance. First, represented module advisors are indeed engaged in management activity. They spend an average of almost 29 percent of each day managing production. This includes "firefighting, troubleshooting, dealing with production bottlenecks, dealing with equipment failures and downtime, expediting, direction to teams on production schedule, record keeping, and giving work assignments." Second, represented and non-represented module advisors differ in their use of time. The differences in the first four categories (production, people, training, and administration) are statistically significant. Represented module advisors spend significantly more time managing people problems: "attendance, manpower, counseling, listening to team members, resolving personnel conflicts, morale building, representing people's needs." Represented module

Table 3-2. Comparison of Represented and Non-Represented Module Advisor Mean Time Use

	Represented Advisor	Non-Represented Advisor	T-Statistic	N
Managing people	0.342	0.259	3.876***	96
Managing production	0.289	0.383	3.213**	96
Training	0.041	0.025	2.065**	96
Administration	0.071	0.05	2.099**	96
Managing costs	0.029	0.04	1.423	96
Problem solving	0.015	0.009	1.381	96
Meetings	0.149	0.159	0.775	96
Other	0.042	0.051	0.755	96

*Significant at the .10 level.
**Significant at the .05 level.
***Significant at the .01 level.

advisors also spend more time on training and administration: "review and analysis of performance data, helping teams track performance, hiring, and team leader development." Non-represented module advisors spend significantly more time on production but also spend almost 26 percent of their time managing people problems.

The balance between time spent on production management and time spent managing people problems is key in evaluating the Saturn partnership arrangement. The data show a relationship between quality performance and a more balanced division of labor than in a traditional division, in which management deals with production as would a supervisor and the union with people problems as would a committeeman. The Saturn partnership agreement calls for the union to take responsibility for business performance and for management to make decisions with employees through consensus. The partnership arrangement at the module level requires a balance both between represented and non-represented advisors and between production and people for each individual module advisor. The data show that this individual balance is significant. For the non-represented module advisor, excessive time managing production at the expense of managing people problems has a negative impact on FTQ improvement. Similarly, for the represented module advisor, excessive time on people at the expense of managing production has a significant negative impact on the level of FTQ. The local union at Saturn has indeed taken responsibility for quality performance. Represented module advisors see quality management as part of their jobs, whereas non-represented module advisors who spend a significant amount of time managing people problems improve relationships, which helps in implementing decisions. Furthermore, partners who balance time managing both people and production must work together closely to achieve consensus on areas of joint responsibility. This results in the represented partner acquiring better technical skills and the non-represented partner developing stronger people skills, with both managing more effectively in each area, having a better understanding and appreciation of the other. Furthermore, the close working relationship develops mutual trust and support.

Table 3-3 presents the relationship between quality and the alignment of attitudes and behaviors between the partnered represented and non-represented module advisors in each department. The lower the number, the greater the alignment. Where there is alignment between the partners on priorities, responsibilities, accountability for team perfor-

Table 3-3. Comparisons of Mean Alignment

Modules with High and Low Quality Improvement

	High Quality Improvement	Low Quality Improvement	T-Statistic	N
Alignment on:				
Balance of Production and People	0.548 (0.512)	1.098 (1.008)	1.963*	30
Responsibilities	0.253 (0.352)	0.707 (0.688)	2.521**	34
Priorities	0.455 (0.657)	1.061 (0.628)	2.696**	34
Accountability	0.253 (0.448)	0.460 (0.527)	1.233	34
Tasks	0.657 (0.648)	0.813 (0.735)	0.655	34

Modules with High and Low First-Time Quality (FTQ)

	High FTQ	Low FTQ	T-Statistic	N
Alignment on:				
Balance of Production and People	0.750 (0.735)	1.046 (1.042)	0.87	30
Responsibilities	0.398 (0.445)	0.629 (0.723)	1.134	34
Priorities	0.663 (0.751)	0.943 (0.641)	1.161	34
Accountability	0.265 (0.438)	0.471 (0.542)	1.226	34
Tasks	0.619 (0.626)	0.864 (0.750)	1.04	34

*Significant at the .10 level. (Standard deviations in parentheses.)
**Significant at the .05 level.
***Significant at the .01 level.

mance, work tasks, or balance of time use on production and people, we see higher levels of quality improvement. Alignment by the partners on balance, responsibilities, and priorities was found to be statistically significant. Although not statistically significant, the same pattern of relationships appears for FTQ performance. When we divided the modules into high and low alignment groups, the mean level of FTQ for the high alignment group was 91.7 percent, whereas the low-alignment group averaged 83.8 percent.

When multiple regression techniques were used to analyze these variables, we could explain 30 percent of the variance in FTQ by the communications of the represented module advisor. Furthermore, the overall communications centrality of the represented module advisors, along with their quality-specific communications and alignment on the question of balance, explained more than 53 percent of the variance in quality improvement.

Summary of the Results

We found three groups of variables to have a significant impact on quality performance, both quality improvement and FTQ. These variables were the following:

1. The amount and pattern of communications and coordination activity;
2. The balance of time spent managing people and production;
3. The alignment between the partnered represented and non-represented managers.

Furthermore, represented managers had a higher level of communications and a greater impact on quality performance than did non-represented managers. Using network analysis techniques, we were able to describe and measure a dense communications network built on the union organization throughout Saturn's management structure. We have argued that by providing this communications and coordination infrastructure through the partnership institution, the local union is adding significant economic value.

Conclusion

Four points stand out in our analysis. First, teams are indeed the foundation on which Saturn's successes have been built. We have observed teams and team members who are very highly motivated, knowledgeable, and trained to solve problems and produce high-quality work in their self-directed fashion. The high performance of these teams, however, rests on a deeper and more fragile foundation—a foundation of trust in Saturn and GM to continue providing employment security and a sustained commitment to the partnership principles on which Saturn is based. Rank-and-file workers at Saturn clearly see their future welfare being tied to the success of the enterprise. When they see this threatened, trust declines and so can performance. Remarkably, however, even during periods of labor-management conflict and tense negotiations, the commitment to quality remained strong at the team level. In some ways, the teams we talked with were more determined than ever to prove that they embodied the commitment to quality that has made Saturn successful in the marketplace.

Second, team members have done a good job in solving problems within their control, especially when supported by module advisors who have their priorities aligned, balance the time they spend on people and production issues, and are well linked into the communications networks of their peers across the plant. Saturn has consistently experienced difficulties in making off-line problem solving work, however. Part of this is due to a failure of leadership at the MAC level; part is due to the lack of strategically focused problem solving that characterizes "best practice" in this arena; part may be due to the historically low priority that GM has given to this activity compared with its Japanese competitors; and part is due to the mixed incentives and rewards facing middle managers and engineers whose career opportunities lie more within GM than within Saturn. There may be other reasons for this failure as well, but the stark reality is that the void in this critical form of problem solving has been evident since at least as early as 1992.

The formal decision rings and particularly the two highest-level forums—the MAC and SAC—have been highly variable in their effectiveness. At critical times, both these bodies have taken up pivotal issues, such as the need to reduce costs or to respond to a recall crisis. At other times, however, the groups have stopped meeting altogether (as for a period of time in 1998–1999) or have met only to make decisions that have not been followed through or implemented (as in the case of the decision to implement a new problem-solving process in 1993). Moreover, the three plants, or business units within the Saturn complex, have developed their own cultures that reflect their GM division legacies. Each business unit has closely guarded its autonomy and from time to time has chosen to ignore or block facilitywide directives from MAC or SAC leaders. Thus, developing a strong and effective team-based leadership model and style has been a challenge for managers at Saturn.

Fourth, Saturn has demonstrated that, when working well, it can achieve world-class levels of quality and high productivity, levels better than other GM plants. But sustaining this high level of productivity over time has been a problem. Given Saturn's commitment to employment security, declining production volumes required because of declining sales will lead productivity numbers to fall because the work force is not reduced commensurate with reduced output. But the problem is deeper than that. Performance also declined after 1996, as workers lost trust in Saturn and GM leadership when in the absence of a commitment to a follow-on product for Spring Hill, the decision was made to source the next generation product in Wilmington. In this way, Saturn mirrors what one might expect in a firm in which employees are critical stakeholders whose long-term livelihood depends so heavily on the long-term success of the enterprise.

We now return to a question raised earlier in this chapter: Does the union through the partnership arrangements add value to managerial processes at Saturn? This is a difficult question to answer, given the very nature of the partnership—that is, the essence of the partnership is that union and management representatives work together to achieve integrative (joint gain) solutions to problems or decisions. In this type of co-management process, it is difficult to estimate the independent effects or contributions made by one side of the partnership. Nevertheless, the data reported in this chapter demonstrate that the local union appears to add significant value to the partnership:

First, as union leaders bring substantive expertise and an independent perspective to a problem, they add value by increasing the quality of decisions made in the various joint committees and forums, from shop floor teams to the SAC. We have observed a number of meetings in which union leaders spoke up directly to confront problems that were difficult for managers to voice openly with their superiors. Recall the examples of this noted by our colleague Bob McKersie as far back as 1990. Other examples would be the 1992 bottom-up planning process that brought to the surface 1,150 cost and quality problems and the initiation of an effort to develop an off-line problem-solving process. It was the union that brought up each of these issues and maintained the pressure. Moreover, the presence of union leaders ensures that human resource dimensions of strategic and operational issues are considered in making decisions.

Second, once decided, the commitment of the union leaders helps to get decisions implemented effectively. The middle-management partnering, the 1992 operating plan, and the extremely successful new model launches in recent years all illustrate the union's implementation ability.

Third, whereas UAW members and leaders have severed their ties to the GM seniority and transfer system and therefore see their long-term security tied solely to Saturn's future, most managers and engineering professionals retain their links to GM. Some managers may have conflicting loyalties between the interests of Saturn and their long-term careers, which they see tied to their functional or technical discipline at GM. As evidenced by the turnover in business team leaders (plant managers) cited above, to some extent it is the union that provides continuity, as well as a site-wide and long-term perspective.

Finally, the institution of individual partnerships between UAW and non-represented Saturn employees throughout the line and staff organizations has created a unique system of co-management. Quality performance appears to be related to the alignment between the partners, as well as communication levels and the individual balancing of production and people management. In all these dimensions, represented managers show a significant impact on quality. This combination of union and management leadership brings important and varied expertise, experience, and perspectives to bear on both the social and technical problems of production.

All these new roles, however, require a different style of management (e.g., greater power sharing, willingness to deal with conflicts and upward communications of problems, greater skill in negotiations and conflict resolution). New styles of union leadership are also required (e.g., more membership participation and communications, more varied approaches to negotiations and the use of power and influence, greater expertise in planning and in the technical issues of management and engineering, skill in balancing new managerial roles with traditional responsibilities and member expectations for representation). As this chapter reveals, neither Saturn managers nor UAW leaders have perfected their new roles. Instead, Saturn serves as a laboratory in which management and labor are learning by doing, sometimes successfully, sometimes not.

In short, the strengths of the Saturn organization as we observed it are in the incredible resource that the teams provide, in the responsiveness of a dense communications and coordination network, and in the one-on-one partnerships that both solve problems in a balanced way and institutionalize and add value to the multiple stakeholder objectives on which Saturn is based. The challenges lie in managing a team-based culture and a consultative structure in ways that still provide the direction, focus, follow-through, and discipline needed to achieve high levels of performance. The quantitative data on the module advisors' impact on quality performance show how this can be accomplished. The key is to generate a dense network of informal communication that supports problem solving and that balances the management of people and production issues among partners who share a common vision of their job. We return to this later, but first we must ask the following: How does the local union create these dense networks and balance its role as a strategic and operational partner in the governance and management of the business, at the same time representing the interests of its members, individually and collectively, when required to do so? It takes a "Different Kind of Union" to perform these functions, as we will examine.

4

Reinventing the Local Union

C onsider two seemingly paradoxical events. In April 1999, after leading the Saturn Spring Hill, Tennessee, UAW local throughout its first twelve years, Mike Bennett, the most vocal and articulate spokesman for the partnership, was defeated in a union election by challengers who promised to be more responsive to rank-and-file concerns. A month later, Suman Bohm, the shop chair of the Saturn Wilmington, Delaware, UAW local and an equally vocal and articulate defender of a more traditional adversarial arms-length model of union-management relations, was defeated by a challenger who promised to develop a stronger partnership with plant management.

How do we interpret these seemingly conflicting developments? A simple interpretation is that democracy works. This is true, but we think they have a deeper implication: Union leaders need to find the right *balance* between their roles as shop floor advocates of rank-and-file members' individual interests and problems and their roles in representing members' collective interests and responsibilities in strategic-level co-management partnership structures and processes. Indeed, based on what we observed at Saturn over the years, we suggest that achieving and sustaining the right balance across a number of different roles and functions is a critical capability of the leaders of the type of new local union observed here.

The local union at Saturn Spring Hill has struggled for years to define its multiple roles in representing and defending the contractual interests of its members while at the same time it participates in running the business. To do this, it has had to reinvent the local union, and in the process, union leaders encountered significant internal tensions and conflicts, as well as conflicts with leaders of its parent international union. This is not surprising, because there is a long history of similar internal conflicts and political battles associated with earlier efforts to sustain union-management partnerships or cooperative efforts.[1] Yet, if shared governance arrangements are to survive, unions will have to manage these conflicts and adapt their internal governance and organizational structures to effectively balance their roles as representatives of individual members' interests, their relationships with national union leaders and sister locals, and their roles in the management and governance processes of the firm. In this chapter, we review how the union at Saturn has adapted to these roles and draw out the capacities that union leaders need to develop if they are to sustain this type of local union model over time.

From the beginning, local union leaders at Saturn defined their role as being responsible for both adding value or contributing to Saturn's economic performance and delivering economic and social benefits to their members. More specifically, the union needed to help Saturn meet the quality, productivity, market share, and profitability targets set by GM, and compete on the levels of its domestic and international competition. At the same time, it needed to achieve for the work force its goals of stable employment with high wages, good working conditions, and an effective voice on the job and in the enterprise, and to meet the expectations the broader community holds for a modern corporation.

In a speech first delivered in 1988 and repeated in public forums many times over the years, Bennett stated that in today's world, long-term employment security cannot be negotiated independent of the economic performance of the firm or solely through collective bargaining after all strategic decisions have been made by management. Rather, his view is that employment security can be achieved only over the long run by both contributing to the economic performance of the firm and participating directly in business planning and decision-making processes to ensure that worker interests are given appropriate consideration.[2]

This formulation of the interests of labor and of the division of responsibility between labor and management is deeply embedded in the structure of Saturn's partnership arrangement, particularly in the one-on-one partnering. While opposition caucuses challenged the incumbent leaders of the local union in elections, in 1993 and again in 1996, none campaigned on a platform of dismantling the partnership. Nor in 1999 did the challengers who defeated Bennett and his caucus run on an anti-partnership platform, contrary to reports in the popular business press. As Ron Hankins, the newly elected president, explained to us, "I am absolutely still committed to it [partnership]." Jeep Williams, the new MAC Advisor and chairman, added, "I am a strong supporter of the partnership—a full partnership, with input and involvement. The membership overwhelmingly want to continue with the partnership process, but they wanted a change in leadership." He emphasized his support for the vision and values of Saturn in his speech after the installation of the new officers at the local union hall: "We all came down here to Saturn because we want to build high-quality cars and have a voice in how to do it. We appreciate the dedicated and hard work the leaders of this union put in to get us here and now we are determined to move forward by strengthening your voice and ensuring Saturn's future."

Meanwhile, in Wilmington, Scott Faraday, the newly elected shop chairman, said, "I want the partnership. I want to help run the business," and Joe Brennan, the local president at Wilmington, explained, "The union is finally headed in a positive direction . . . We need to understand the business. We need to understand what's happening in the plant . . . Every time we get a chance to participate in decision making, I look at it as an opportunity, at least to be in the game."

Thus, the challenge facing the new union leaders is to find the right balance in their roles as co-managers in running the business and as effective advocates for rank-and-file concerns and interests. In this chapter we review the experiences of the Spring Hill local union during its first generation to identify lessons for not only current but also future leaders of this local and for others striving to balance these different responsibilities in other settings.

The New Local Union: Servicing and Internal Organizing

UAW Local 1853 developed a number of new approaches to serving both the traditional and the newer functions called for by its role in the partnership. Most of these approaches focused on internal organizing of its members to support their greater participation and input in their jobs and their union. The key innovations are listed in Figure 4-1.

Congress was formed in 1988 and is unique to Saturn. It is a forum in which the union leaders meet with module advisors and all other union

Congress: Twice-a-month meetings attended by all local union executive board members, union module advisors, crew coordinators, and other key staff functional coordinators. The purpose of the Congress is to provide the local union with strategic direction and focus on specific issues, mostly related to the state of the business and the roles these representatives played in co-managing it.

Leadership Team: Approximately 50 top union leaders, including elected officers, Executive Board members, and crew coordinators. It meets every week and conducts periodic workshops to discuss the partnership, union strategy, and business issues.

Work Unit Counselors: Bi-monthly meetings are held between elected union officers and elected Work Unit counselors to discuss their roles and responsibilities as both production team leaders and elected union representatives.

Block Meetings: Weekly meetings between module advisors, Work Unit counselors, and crew coordinators to provide communications and discuss operating problems and issues in each module.

Rap Sessions: Monthly meetings held in each Business Team between the local union president and union members in an open question and answer forum.

Town Hall: Monthly local union meetings held twice during the normal work day to facilitate the participation by crews on both first and second shifts.

Member to Member Survey: An annual survey that utilizes the team leaders to conduct interviews with every individual union member on the issues, concerns, or needs they would like to see addressed by the union.

Figure 4-1. Participatory processes used by the local union.

members holding jointly selected positions in the partnership to share information and discuss issues ranging from the partnership problems to corporate performance. During one such meeting in April 1992, Congress received the same detailed briefing on Saturn's financial performance and 1993 final budget that earlier that week had been given to Lloyd Reuss, the GM president. The top union leadership had participated in the budget generation at earlier stages. All UAW partners are required to attend this several-hour meeting, which is held twice a month.

From time to time, leadership team meetings have been held to discuss pending issues and challenges facing the business, the local, or both. For example, during 1992, in response to increasing financial pressure on Saturn to break even, union leaders met to decide what steps were needed to improve the union's management of the business. They used a series of off-site workshops (we attended some held in a barn not far from Spring Hill) to develop a team-directed business plan for improving Saturn's operating performance and a plan to change the partnership assignments of union leaders in the different business units. Another such "off-site" was called by Williams and Hankins in June 1999, four days after they were sworn into office, to discuss how they and their fellow officers would begin to respond to their mandate from the membership.

The UAW used member-to-member surveys at a number of critical junctures, such as when the contract comes up for renewal or other critical problems arise requiring leadership action. The 1991 member-to-member survey, for example, served as the basis for the union's negotiating platform in the contract renewal process that year. Similar member-to-member surveys were conducted before negotiations in 1994, and provided important data on membership preferences that were critical in resolving a debate between local and international union leaders over the contract provisions governing shift assignments, work schedules, and several other issues. Because the member-to-member surveys involve personal interviews by UAW leaders of individual members, they allow members to raise issues that otherwise would not be introduced in formal written questionnaire surveys, local union meetings, or traditional grievance procedures. They also reinforce the principle that part of the job of a team leader and union leader is to encourage this type of upward communication on an ongoing basis.

The other processes listed in Figure 4-1—meetings of work unit counselors, block meetings of other leaders in specific parts of the plant, and rap sessions involving local union leaders and rank-and-file members—

are built into the union's ongoing calendar of events. Visitors to Saturn are likely to see videos of one of these sessions, or the local union Town Hall (membership meeting), broadcast on monitors in the cafeteria or other public spaces throughout the facility. More recently, the local has created its own web site and has a staff member assigned to posting daily updates for members on issues ranging from business developments to social and political events within the local and in the outside world.

These processes are designed to extend the principles of participation embedded in Saturn's organizational design to the administration of the local union. Shifting to this type of leadership style has been one of the biggest changes required of local union leaders in organizations that promote teamwork and employee participation.[3] The Saturn local has created a comprehensive and sophisticated infrastructure to support these new roles.

As new problems have surfaced, the local union has experimented with a number of approaches to its internal structure. For the first few years, the focus of the partnership was necessarily on designing and building the organization. In 1990, with the start of production, however, the priority shifted to building cars. Making the transition from organization building to automobile building challenged the union and required adjustments in the partnership arrangements. After recognizing that the SAC, MAC, and business unit decision rings were insufficient avenues for co-managing the business, the union initiated the idea of one-on-one partnering. Furthermore, team leaders become union officials after their election. Therefore, their responsibilities include both team coordination as well as representing members' needs at some level. This has never been an easy assignment, as evidenced by data on team leader turnover. Ten percent of the team leaders elected in February 1992 had resigned by October of that year. By 1995 the number of elected team leaders had risen to 700. When elected team leaders, crew coordinators, and union officials are added to the 400 jointly selected UAW partners, almost 1 member in 5 has a position of leadership in the union. This represents an extremely high level of membership participation in the leadership ranks of the local union.

Comparison with Other United Auto Workers Locals

The net effect of the governance and co-management structures at Saturn is that union members and leaders serve in a wider variety of roles than their counterparts in other locals. Elected officers sit on the SAC and MAC and are partnered with executives and plant managers, and crew coordinators (committeemen) are partnered with non-represented coordinators who cover entire shifts as superintendents do in traditional GM plants. Furthermore, more than 400 jointly selected union members have partnership roles ranging from module advisors engaged in daily operations management with their non-represented counterparts to partnerships with management involved in supplier and retailer selection, marketing and public relations, product development, choice of new technology, ergonomics and safety, training and development, performance appraisal, information systems, and operations management. In addition, through weekly participation in off-line decision rings at the corporate, manufacturing site, and plant levels, the union participates in operations' decision making and business planning. Furthermore, the union is involved in personnel selection because all hiring recommendations come from the teams themselves.

Traditionally, UAW local unions would have formal input into very few of these decisions. Leaders in other parts of the UAW, however, are increasingly getting involved in joint efforts and are participating informally in a wide variety of discussions and decisions that in the past would have been held confidential by management. For example, an international union leader responsible for a key division of the union noted at a recent conference that, in order to feel he can effectively represent his members' interests, he needs to know what products the plants he is responsible for might be bidding on at least two years into the future. Only by having this information early could he work with management to discuss changes that would increase the chances of getting the flow of products needed to ensure long-term job security for his members. Similarly, in recent years the UAW and American automakers have implemented a variety of joint programs ranging from safety and health committees, large and well-funded joint training programs, employee involvement processes, and so forth.[4] Figure 4-2 presents, for example, the long list of joint programs administered by the UAW and GM Joint Human Resources Center. In his discussions with us, UAW Vice President Richard Shoemaker stressed that the Saturn local has far more formal roles and responsibilities for participation and co-management than sister locals. Other locals, however, are engaged in similar efforts on a more limited scale and agenda and in more informal and varied ways. So although the Saturn local has the most extensive net-

Apprenticeship Training
Attendance Programs
Child Care
Communication Systems
Contract Bidding
Dislocated Employee Training and Placement
Elimination of Double Standards (parking, cafeteria, pay check
    distribution, clock cards)
Employee Benefit Program Administration
Employee Involvement Process (EI, QC, QWL, etc.)
Enhanced Educational Programs
Ergonomics
Health & Safety
Health Care Cost Containment
Improvement in the Quality of Product &/or Service
Introduction of New Technology
Joint Legislative Lobbying re: Jointly Supported Issues
Long Term Health Care
New Business Ventures
New Hire Orientation
Open House Programs
Pension Fund Investment
Prepaid Legal Services
Pre-Retirement Planning
Production Scheduling
Selection of Colleges/Universities for Rendering Services
Selection of Outside Consultants for EI process, etc.
Skill Development & Training
Supervisor Ratios
Tuition Assistance/Basic Education
United Fund Drives
Wellness Programs

Figure 4-2. Labor-management joint implementation of negotiated provisions.
(Source: United Auto Workers.)

work of formal roles built into its structure and the co-management process, it should not be viewed as completely distinct from what its sister
locals are attempting to do.

Moreover, unions representing workers in other industries increasingly find themselves involved in similar informal and, sometimes, formal joint processes, co-management roles, or both. This was clearly
pointed out by discussions that took place among a wide range of local
union leaders at a recent conference at Rutgers University. As one local
union leader from the aerospace industry put it,

> I think that traditionally as a union leader, you'd rather be called a bas-
> tard than a manager sometimes. I mean that's like an inbred thing that I
> inherited from my family. But I think it snuck up on [me] . . . Whether
> you realize it or not, [whether] you get compensated for it or not, you are
> a manager. You know you manage. I'm like a human resource person in
> my plant, and I do take part [in] discussions with the upper manage-
> ment. My function there as a manager is trying to influence the company
> to control their amount of production and how they use my labor force
> that I'm responsible for. And you know whether I get compensated like
> big CEOs and everybody else, I'm as much of a manager there at that
> plant, and in my department . . . I have six hundred workers in there, and
> every day I'm part of a decision-making process with the company on
> how they're going to use those people, how many are they going to use,
> how many of them have to be laid off and why, and how many of them
> have to be called back from layoff and why. So, whether I like to admit it
> or not, we are co-managers there; that's what this team work stuff has
> done to us. You know, it's turned me into a middle manager.

The experiences at Saturn should prove useful to other local leaders
as they decide how to respond to the need to be more involved formally
or informally in joint governance and co-management processes.

Negotiations and Grievance Handling

The local union at Saturn is responsible for the traditional roles of
contract negotiations and grievance handling. Typically, UAW locals
handle negotiations through an elected bargaining committee. Although
the local union at Saturn has an elected bargaining committee, it relies
heavily on member-to-member surveys to set priorities and objectives
for negotiations. For example, the member-to-member survey that pre-

ceded 1994 negotiations showed that absenteeism and representation issues were high-priority membership concerns and therefore needed to be addressed.

UAW locals normally handle grievances through an elected grievance committee, with approximately one committeeman for every 250 members. Before 1995, at Saturn only the local union president or vice presidents could write grievances. In late 1994, the contract was changed to provide for fourteen elected crew coordinators who could file and handle grievances. Even so, the ratio of members to crew coordinators is over 520 to 1, and emphasis is placed on solving problems at the lowest level possible before they escalate to the point at which they are filed as formal grievances. After the crew coordinator role was established to handle grievances, we were asked by the union and company to design and lead a series of workshops for the coordinators and other union and management leaders focused on mutual gains' approaches and tools for conflict resolution and problem solving.

The contrast between Local 1853 and other UAW locals is important for three reasons. First, it illustrates the multitude of opportunities, both off-line and on-line, by which the local leaders at Saturn can represent member interests in significant management decisions. The expectation is that the incorporation of worker input early in the decision-making process will result in better decisions that reflect labor's collective interests, as well as more effective implementation. Second, it illustrates the difference in resource allocation between the Saturn local and other UAW locals. The Saturn local has devoted most of its organization and resources to its management and governance roles, and it has approximately half the number of grievance filers that a more traditional UAW local its size would have. Third, one trend in labor-management relations today is for union leaders in many locals to take on more active co-management responsibilities in a range of emerging joint activities, and the Saturn local may simply be a prominent model of one type of local union of the future—an example that can provide both positive and negative lessons from which others can learn and improve upon.

External Organizing and the Amalgamation of the Local

From the beginning, local leaders sought to expand the representation of the union to Saturn contract workers. To date, two additional

UAW units have been added to the original local union. The first incorporates approximately 120 employees of the Morrison Milco Food Service, a contractor that runs Saturn's four on-site cafeterias. The second unit includes 240 employees of the Premier Corporation, which provides services to Saturn for paint booth cleaning, janitorial services, on-site grounds keeping, and auto drive-away for vehicle transportation loading. These amalgamated units of UAW Local 1853 participate in local-wide elections. The local also organized the 600 direct material truck drivers of the Ryder Corporation, whose members voted to form their own independent UAW local.

This amalgamation expands the membership base of the union and provides representation to workers who in most firms remain unorganized and are treated as second-class citizens. It also adds a greater diversity of interests to the local union and, by extension, to Saturn. Giving voice to these interests allows these workers to surface their concerns. In 1993 the cafeteria workers went on strike, primarily over wage issues. Although their wages had improved considerably since joining the UAW, they were still well behind their brothers and sisters in the production and maintenance units. The strike lasted several weeks, with picket lines set up in the plant at the doors of the cafeteria rather than at the front gate, which would have closed down production because members of the production and maintenance unit refused to cross the line. (Visitors to the plant during the strike had the opportunity to sample from a variety of home-cooked cuisines, ranging from Wisconsin-style bratwurst to Texas barbecue to Mexican tortillas that reflected the diverse geographic origins of the work force and the shared spirit of making do while their brothers and sisters in the cafeteria were on strike.) A resolution came only after the local union leadership induced Saturn management to put pressure on Morrison Milco for a settlement.

Local Union Infrastructure for High-Performance Manufacturing

One of our early impressions of Saturn's manufacturing operations was that the organization had a tremendous capacity to spread information rapidly across the three plants. We also had the sense that much of this communication system was built on the union organization. In visits to other unionized manufacturing plants, we often heard managers and union members comment that the union gets information before middle management and supervision. This appeared to be true at Saturn as well. Furthermore, UAW members in managerial assignments were in a position to do something with the information they received.

For example, the following illustration shows the unique role the union plays in communication. In May 1993, as we were preparing to administer surveys to module advisors on their managerial behaviors and priorities, time use, and communications, the MAC announced the date in June for the separation of a third crew (called C crew) from A and B crews. The separation also meant the decisions on new assignments and promotions for C crew module advisor positions had been made. When we became aware that announcements of the new assignments and promotions were to be released, we approached the union president. We explained our concern that once people found out about their new positions they might not answer the surveys the same way, because some would focus their attention on their new jobs and others on the fact that they were not getting the new assignments they had requested. Some were even scheduled to leave their old jobs and begin training in their new ones before they would get the surveys.

Because the MAC had a great deal of interest in this research and had sanctioned the surveys, the local president immediately directed, through his network of UAW partners, that no announcement of new assignments be made. Within the hour, the word had circulated all three plants, and all reassignments, promotions, and training for C crew leadership were held up for several weeks until we could complete all survey work without compromising the reliability of the data.

A second example of effective communication was reported to us in the aftermath of the 1998 negotiations. Through the year, rumors have been circulating at Saturn about GM's new "Yellowstone" strategy to divide the assembly process into discrete modules and outsource as many as possible. A number of Saturn leaders, including several union module advisors, were invited to join a trip to Detroit for a briefing that included Yellowstone. On their return, they presented the information at Congress. The non-represented managers had no similar forum, so as union leaders rolled the information out to their team leaders, many people on the floor had more information than did their non-represented leaders. Sometimes, however, information flows the other way as well. For example, we were told in a January 1999 interview with module advisors that when a non-represented manager recently visited a

GM Yellowstone project in Brazil, he was invited to brief Congress on his return: "He came back and the first people he shared his information with were the UAW Congress. He didn't have an avenue to come back and tell the non-represented leaders."

We view this local union as a dense social network that creates the communications and coordination that not only build the local union but also support high-performance manufacturing. These organizational activities are what undergird the network of day to day on-line problem-solving activities discussed earlier with both the qualitative and quantitative data. But they also pose some challenges to the union's ability to represent its members. A look at the internal political dynamics of this local union shows the need for the union to balance its co-management role with effective internal political processes and individual and collective representation.

Balancing Act: Partnership and Shop Floor Representation

This system of co-management and joint governance has presented enormous challenges for the local union, because it puts the new partnership relations in tension with the traditional forms of representation that union members formerly experienced in their local unions. These tensions fall into two broad categories: those internal to the local and those between the local and the national union.

Internal tensions have developed within the rank and file over concerns about individual representation. Tensions have also developed within the local leadership over access to the new forms of power created by the partnership. This second dilemma has to do with the selection process for union leaders who fill the on-line management positions in the partnership. Until 1995, the union and company jointly selected all of these representatives. The evidence presented in Chapter 3 suggests that it would have been difficult to achieve Saturn's level of quality performance with a more traditional system of elected grievance committeemen and non-represented supervisors. But, pressures for better representation of individual member interests built up in this system and led to the election of the union's crew coordinators to provide more traditional representation and grievance handling. A key question for the local union is how the tension between a joint-selection process to fill key management positions and a process by which the members themselves elect their represented managers will be worked out.

External tensions also have developed with the UAW International and GM over questions of local autonomy and divergence from national union policies and corporate practices. These grew out of the generic conflicts that result from a local union exercising greater autonomy as it engages in a new arena of decision making and the national union seeking to preserve solidarity, consistency in practices across locals, and protection from whipsawing through adherence to national bargaining patterns. These issues are also expressions of the natural tension between the independence necessary for innovation and the corporate tendency toward centralization.[5] Over the past few years, Saturn has experienced an erosion of its independence in decision making, as GM has moved it toward convergence with other models in a common platform while centralizing decisions on supplier selection, new products, and capital for capacity expansion.

Tensions over Representation

A variety of data suggest that the question of the local union's ability to provide adequate representation under the new partnership arrangement has been an issue at Saturn. During the 1993 local elections (the second in Saturn's history), one of several competing caucuses ran on a platform of increased representation through direct election (in a fashion consistent with the UAW tradition for shop committee representatives) of all 400 full-time represented managers. Those positions were filled by a joint selection process, as were the positions of all non-represented (i.e., salaried management) partners. Bennett, the union president at that time, believed that elections for all positions would politicize the partnership, diminishing the ability of these individuals to balance the needs of people with the needs of the business, and that popularity, not skills, knowledge, and ability, would become the dominant qualification. He and others on the local executive board argued that politicizing the process would lead to a return of the old grievance committee structure, an increase in adversarialism, and a movement away from consensus decision making and joint problem solving. If excluded from the selection process, management would likely select more traditional non-represented supervisors as a counterpart, with no union input in selection.

Accordingly, the local union leaders sought to continue the process of joint selection by management and union representatives. A referendum on the question of electing crew coordinators and module advisors took place in early 1993, with 71 percent of the membership voting to continue the process of joint selection. This vote appeared to reaffirm the commitment of the majority of the rank and file to the principles underlying the Saturn partnership. Internal tensions over this question continued, however.

In the spring of 1993, the local union election resulted in a runoff, with the president and his executive board being returned to office after a close race. Nevertheless, the issue of appropriate representation continued to surface. The local conducted a member-to-member survey in the summer of 1993 to gain a deeper understanding of these concerns. Nearly 6,000 members (approximately 90 percent of the membership) were interviewed. Representation was one of the top ten issues raised, with 31 percent of the membership raising it as a concern. A majority of these respondents complained that "they had not seen their elected representatives since the elections and wanted to see them more often," and the question of electing the jointly selected union representatives was raised again. Another frequent complaint dealt with whether union leaders were performing their duty of fair representation. Concern was expressed about the "need for consistent interpretation and application of the Memo of Agreement and Guiding Principles" by different union leaders.

Specifically, the application of the attendance policy was seen as unfair or inequitable and was the top issue raised in the survey. It was mentioned by almost 50 percent of those surveyed by the union. When work teams were originally organized, they were empowered with the authority to manage absenteeism and implement attendance guidelines. As the number of work units grew to 700, however, problems of inconsistency arose. A common practice in one work unit might be a violation in another. Members expressed concern that discipline for absenteeism was not being handled in an equitable way. The local union leadership saw the member-to-member results as a call for stricter guidelines or enforcement of current policy. The union led an effort to develop new companywide attendance guidelines and put them to a vote by the membership in 1994. Although the new policy adopted by the membership resulted in the lowest noncontractual (casual, unexcused) absenteeism in GM (at 0.25 percent, Saturn is reported to have less than half of GM's average), individuals could now be disciplined for behaviors previously accepted in their module. As a result, members increasingly expressed the need for individual representation, even though their collective interests were represented (through the local union) in both drafting the policy and ratifying it through a referendum.

We conducted a series of ten focus group interviews in May and June 1994 to gain a deeper understanding of members' concerns over representation and of their views of the role the union was playing in the partnership. Participants were randomly selected, from all crews and business units. The comments of individual members that follow highlight both the common themes that emerged and the differences in point of view.

Representing Members' Collective Interests

Most of the members interviewed saw value in the representation by the local of their collective interests in business decision making, and they approved of this aspect of the union's performance.

> I believe we're seeing a lot of input. One thing we said early on is, as UAW members, we have a heck of a lot of power around here. We can change some decisions and make decisions. But, better have your information correct and your ducks in a row. You need to be right. And if you do, if you are right in what you think the decision can be or should be, you can buck the management folks and change it. And I've been part of doing some of that.

> We're quite proud of the fact that the whole shop was put together from ground up and organized by UAW and runs today with UAW people only. We do not have any input from any management folks on daily affairs.

> There is somebody [union leader] out here looking [out] for me and all these other folks, and they're gonna be up there with the MAC and SAC making those decisions.

> A good example [is] job setup. The teams are going through workshops setting up their jobs to be efficient. In the old days [at GM], the engineers used to do the time studies, and everything used to be dictated—"This is your job." If you felt your job was overloaded, you'd write a grievance on it and send it in. And here [at Saturn] . . . the teams have people they designate to go represent them [across] all three crews, and they go to the workshop and they do the timing and jobs and the layouts and everything to try to make the job efficient. So it's good for business, but it's not going to kill the people.

More of the way that our system of representation works though is in a form of information sharing, more than representing you [individually] and your interests. We know more about the business than probably we ever have.

Most of the members interviewed on this issue did not have complaints with the representation of collective interests by local leadership in making business decisions. Although some showed a lack of knowledge about what actually takes place at the SAC, MAC, and business unit decision rings, many were satisfied with the union's influence on strategic level decision making.

Representation as Individual Advocacy

Although members accepted the value of collective representation at the strategic level, their primary concern was a perceived lack of individual representation by union officials. Workers on the floor often value representation for violations of individual rights, day-to-day injustices, or unequal treatment more than input into broader strategic questions. This form of representation can be thought of as a sense of personal advocacy and due process. Many members had experienced this kind of representation at GM—although there was often an assumption that an injury to one was an injury to all—where grievance committee members could always be relied on to fight for individual members' rights and interests.

Members compared the visible presence of the committeeman in GM with the lack of visible representation at Saturn. Many were looking for accessible advocates who could write grievances for them if they believed treatment was inequitable or unfair. There were complaints of inadequate representation to ensure equity and due process after decisions and policies were made. Examples included the consultation (discipline) process (e.g., fear about job loss), inability to get questions answered and decisions made, and inconsistency or favoritism in treatment by module advisors (e.g., staffing reductions, transfers). Furthermore, many members believed that they should be able to elect a greater number of the union partners to enhance individual advocacy. Although various alternatives to the traditional committeeman structure were discussed, all included the election of representatives. Some saw this as a way to increase authority when dealing with non-represented module advisors, because elected representatives would be directly responsible to a constituency. Team members also expressed a desire for more direct and visible communications with union leaders and for more opportunities for bottom-up input. Managing conflict within the team was a concern for some:

> Without having supervisors here, you're left to . . . deal with your own conflict, to manage [our]selves and watch over and make sure everybody does right . . . Most part people here fare pretty good. But . . . it's really hard for people to deal with certain types of team issues. When . . . somebody's really screwing up, we got to deal with setting this person straight. Some teams may be doing okay in that. But it has been my experience that a lot of teams would rather have somebody else deal with that in the way that the supervisor used to.

Members varied in their desire for the type of representation they experienced in GM:

> As far as the old world, I'd never had to have someone represent me. But it was nice to know that there was somebody there to hear if you were ever in trouble . . .

> I'm not sure if it has anything to do with consistency, because that's been a big word around here, consistency. And I don't believe in consistency. I think you should have individuals, you know, each team can do something different, and they want everyone to do the same exact things, and we have nothing but conflict. We could call your representative in to settle the conflict. They're not there like the committeemen used to be. The committeemen used to back you up if you were wrong. I don't think I'm looking for a committeeman.

> I hated [the] old world. When I saw the union representative helping the troublemaker all the time, I hated that. And, I don't ever want to see that come back, but I do want some representation. Something that you can count on, that you know will be there to help you if there is a problem.

> I just want to say, we're doing a lot of good things. We're doing a lot of positive things. And we can fix the system we got here without going back completely to the old system . . . You don't have to go back to the old committeemen system; you don't have to do that. But, bottom line, you have to have a procedure or a system in place to address grievances.

Team members also believed that team leaders were not sufficiently trained or empowered to represent them.

You want to call [the team leader] your first line of representation? He's got too much other stuff to do. He's out there building cars. He's running the meetings . . . You need somebody [whose] job is to represent people out there on the floor, not to build cars, not to be chasing down that other stuff somebody's got him doing. He needs to take care of people . . . only the people. They're doing too much. They don't have time to represent you.

Team members also reported frustration that they could not grieve decisions the union itself was party to—for example, the attendance policy.

Last week I went to the union office, and I said I wanted to write a grievance. I was told that I couldn't write a grievance because the decisions made were not solely management . . . they were union and management. So, therefore, you cannot write a grievance. . . . When I was told that I couldn't write a grievance, I thought, "Well, what am I paying union dues for?"

Members were confused about the managerial and representational roles and responsibilities of the union partners. Often represented module advisors were not seen as adequate representatives, because they were perceived as too business- and production-focused and were lacking authority because they are were not elected by the membership they would represent. In addition, module advisors were often involved in the very issues for which members were seeking representation. For example, cuts and displacements in team staffing and the consultation (discipline) process typically involved module advisors.

I would say that neither one [represented or non-represented module advisors] are doing any real representing. They're just trying to sort out the problems and give you their idea, their point of view.

As far as the represented or the non-represented module advisor, and I've heard this lately, they are not your union representative, they are represented by the union. It makes a difference. They're not like a committeeman. They are in the union, they represented their union, but they are not your union representative. You gotta understand that.

The committeeman [in my old GM plant], he just called and listened to what your problem was or what was going on, catch the story from the other side, and then represent you. And the system we have here where you don't have a committeeman, you have the same person to represent you as is usually involved in the problem also. So that tends to make it biased. I mean, if you have a problem and you go talk to the module advisor about it . . . you don't have . . . any neutral ground here, nobody neutral to listen to both sides and help you out.

Team members, however, also expressed contradictory views of the effectiveness of module advisor representation.

I think they [represented module advisors] put in a little bit more of a fight for something that you want. They really hear you out. They hear what you have to say.

I have one module advisor that's represented, and I think he's one of the best we have. He is concerned about people. And he stays around us, he communicates with us, and he talks to us, and he's a good representative to us.

Another perspective on this issue of representation and advocacy was provided by a focus group of represented module advisors. Some of them commented that the problem was that team members wanted the traditional grievance committeemen they had under GM.

People are accustomed to committeemen to be able to write a grievance. We're not set up on that same system, and that's where the problems are occurring. We have a lot of people here who have a lot of seniority, and they're accustomed to that committeeman being right there to answer whatever their call may be; petty or whatever, they're used to him being there, writing a grievance regardless of what it is. They want that grievance written, even if it's not even worth writing. They want that because they got that at their old plant.

I consider myself a resource to the people, and the object is if they've got an issue, it's up to [me] to help them resolve it. It may not always be to their satisfaction, and I think that's where the committeemen keeps coming up, because a lot of people feel that "because it doesn't come out my way, then I want a committeeman." The committeeman still couldn't assure them that the grievance would come out in their favor.

Other module advisors believed that they were solving individual members' problems through a channel other than the grievance procedure.

As resources to them . . . we get the matter resolved. Now it's not through the grievance process all the time. You don't have to have a grievance to solve every issue. You get them tied in with the right people. You direct them in the right direction, get the information for them, and they'll still come up with the same results.

We are like committeemen, but we just don't have that name . . . because first of all, we do grieve whatever it is, but we don't put it all down on paper. It's just in a different perspective of how we handle it . . . whereas we don't file a grievance, we try to deal with the issue and resolve it where it will be a win-win for all of us.

Finally, module advisors believed that, although they wanted to solve problems for team members, they could not represent them if they were in violation of policies that the union supported or participated in creating.

There are certain things that I can do and there are certain things that I cannot do because I must always remember that I have to represent that team member. If the team member's wrong, I sit down and tell them, "You know, that wasn't right; you shouldn't have done that." But I can't sit up and know somebody did something wrong and try to make it so that they don't get in trouble. I can't do that.

I tell them that I represent. If you've got an issue, then I'll find out what your issue is. I'll find out the resources that need to be involved, and we'll go from there. If you are wrong, I'll let you know you're wrong. If something that you did was not appropriate, then I'll let you know that. Some people want to do wrong, and they want you to say it's okay.

As a represented module advisor, we can have a decision that was made, let's just say people leaving early. I'm not going to stand at the back door, or stand in the alley way, or stand in the parking lot, looking at seeing who leaves. My [non-represented] partner will. If my partner catches them, and they know they're not supposed to leave, that's it . . . I'm supposed to stop them before they get to that door. That's my job.

You still can grieve; if someone still wants a grievance, you can still go through the process through the vice president and have them do that for you.

Members expressed frustration about the selection process for full-time union positions in the partnership, which was seen by some members as creating a new privileged class within the local. There appeared to be a perception among some members that the joint selection process for partnered positions (module advisors and other jointly selected partnership positions) is not strictly merit or skill based and that politics plays a role. Because approximately 400 full-time jobs for union partners are filled through the joint selection process, the stakes are high.

> I believe it's a power struggle: those who are in charge and those who wish to be. You get up there, you get a lot of power. You get hundreds of people below you appointed. You're going to get their support. Just about any issue that comes through. If you were looking for a leadership position and you didn't go along with your top UAW leadership with that viewpoint, personally [I'm] not so sure of what your chances are of receiving that job.

> You've got to take politics out of it, and if you've got somebody on the floor that's in a leadership position or whatever position and they're disagreeing with you, you don't remove them because they're disagreeing with what you're saying. . . . And the only way that is going to happen is to take it out of political appointment and let the people elect them.

> [The union leadership] has too much power . . . cronies everywhere, and they . . . got their little cushy job. Half of them don't rotate. They're not going to buck the system. There's too much power at that level here. If you started electing people, people will elect people to represent them. It will be a people's place again.

Comparing Saturn with General Motors

Members voiced support as well as criticism of the impact of the partnership arrangements on the union membership. Although there appear to be serious questions regarding the forms of representation, the majority of those interviewed strongly preferred the Saturn partnership arrangements and team-based work system to that of GM and did not want to return to the system used by GM.

> I came to Saturn as my plant was announcing it was closing. But I like the fact that down here we rotate jobs. And everybody at least on our team is encouraged to pull their share. You got a bad job one day and a good job the [next]. Nobody has to do the same jobs. It's not like somebody's got a cushy job all day like the other [plants].

> The structure here is good. In implementing the structure there are rough roads. I would [say] that 85 percent of it I prefer. There are possibly areas that we need to improve on, and I imagine that will be an ongoing thing.

We're never going to get it perfect. I prefer this structure. Even though it has errors [that] gotta be roughed out a while, I prefer this.

From what I'm used to [at GM] the business had a supervisor for every thirty people or so. With our system, how many people we have in a module, one hundred? And there's two people that are over [us]. They can cover a lot more ground and equal out the business part, the rep and nonrep. They work good together. They see things from different perspectives. The supervisor was mainly concerned with making sure the cars went through the area. That was generally it.

Other team members liked the increased responsibility they could take on through the partnership arrangement, particularly around the issue of manufacturing quality.

I'd have to say that I prefer the way things are now. I feel like we run our own little business in our team. I think the more responsibility we show, the more that you're kind of left on your own to do what you need to do.

This particular process, the partnership, the team concept, it requires more of the worker than old GM work [system]. When I say more I didn't say stress, but I mean overall work and looking at your quality. Old GM world, you went in, found your machine, and you watched your schedule. People say stress. I have not experienced the stress, what I was referring to was responsibility. No, you don't work harder. More responsibility [is] delegated to you.

Quality is not our problem. I have as much right to turn that line off, being nobody, as the represented module advisor. I have that much power in my hand. If I see a quality error and it's bad enough that I don't want to run the line, I have that power. I don't need to ask anybody. My manager cannot make me turn that line on until a viable solution is in place and is in agreement with me. That's what makes this plant successful, by the way.

[Quality's] better because we have a decision to say "No, we're not going to run that crap," "No, these parts aren't clean enough from the vendor." I was in a blower department in [GM]. You guys know what happened— right down the tubes. They were running stuff through there we knew was no good. I'd tell my foreman, "This is not working out. It's not gauging right." He'd say to run it. If you didn't, that was your job.

Finally, some team members, although acknowledging the problems still to be worked out at Saturn, believed the system there represented a step forward that has also brought them a greater sense of dignity.

> [Even with] the conflict and everything we have down here, [it] is still a heck of a place to work. I wish I got here twenty years ago, really, because I can afford a little conflict once in a while. You do have a lot of it, but it's still a good place to work. We are not there in heaven yet. We're not in utopia. It's been a good place to work.

> All in all, this is probably the best place I ever worked. Best, but sometimes it is the most messed-up place. I'd rather work here than to go back to GM.

> So, union has brought a dignity to the work force, and without that dignity the work force wouldn't be able to produce its quality products if they wanted to.

In all ten focus groups, strong support was expressed for the Saturn partnership. This finding is consistent with the 1993 member-to-member survey, which indicated significant satisfaction with the partnership arrangements, 84 percent responding that Saturn was "great" or "headed in the right direction," and only 10 percent stating that it was "headed in the wrong direction" or "I wish I could find another job." Even candidates from opposing caucuses in the union argued that the partnership was preferable to the traditional GM-UAW relationship. As one elected crew coordinator put it,

> At [my old plant] labor relations were more of an adversarial relationship. Management made the decisions, labor worked. If those decisions that management made had an adverse effect on the union, then the union's recourse was to file a grievance. Depending on how severe, it could even get up to a walkout, or plant shutdown, or something like that. At Saturn it is totally the opposite. You have taken that line out, and you have management and labor manage the business. It is becoming more clear on what my role is, and that is represent the stakes and equities of the team members that are out there. In [the management partner's] role, it is looking out for the interest of the business. Then by combining those two and making sure that the business is being taken care of and that the people are being taken care of, you have successfully integrated the two. You'll always need those two. We [have] consensus on those decisions. And some team members don't like those decisions. So, I will go in and sit down and help explain why we made that decision. And they will accept that a lot better from me than from [my partner].

Summary of the Interviews

The overall themes that emerged can be summarized as follows:

- The local union was perceived by its membership as having significant input into strategic, policy, and operating decisions.
- The rank and file, however, did not see this representation as a substitute for the type of individual advocacy they enjoyed under the grievance committee structure of GM.
- When a policy into which the union had input was perceived as inequitable or unfair, the issue of individual member representation became even more acute. This was the case in the disputes over the absenteeism policy.
- The jointly selected union partners were not seen as representatives of individual members. Rather, they were seen as managers who represented the union as an institution in operations decision making. Their role, unlike the role of a grievance committeeman in GM, was not perceived to be that of individual representation or advocacy.
- Concern was expressed about the equity and method by which the union selected members for the full-time partnership positions. The substantial power and influence these selections provide have been a focus for the internal politics of the local as well as the disputes between the local and international union.
- Although individual representation was a concern, support for the partnership structure remained strong, with the vast majority of members expressing preference for Saturn over GM.

Success and Failures in Achieving Balance

Several months after these focus group interviews were conducted, the local conducted its own written survey of 420 randomly selected members. Fifty-three percent reported that they were dissatisfied or very dissatisfied with the current level of representation from the local. This quantitative finding supports the qualitative data reported here.

During negotiations conducted in the fall of 1994, the local modified the contract to allow for 14 union crew coordinators to be elected by the membership in April 1995 with the authority to write grievances. Since the election of crew coordinators, grievance filing has increased significantly. From the period 1988 to 1994, a total of 205 grievances were filed.

In 1995 alone, the first year crew coordinators were elected, 279 grievances were filed. These were followed by 245 grievances in 1996. It is not altogether clear, however, what this increase in grievances represents. As one of the union vice presidents suggested, the increase may indicate that the elected crew coordinators were relying more on grievances to solve problems than did the jointly selected crew coordinators.

> I would say maybe some of those guys are dependent on a grievance to try to resolve an issue [rather] than facilitating disputes between the parties. . . . The other people didn't have that option when they were appointed. They didn't have the option to file a grievance. . . . So, the number of issues is probably an average number that all of them [crew coordinators] were getting. I think the data say some people are using much different ways to resolve the issues than others . . . . The answer is not more [crew coordinators]. . . . We added fourteen and people are still saying [representation] is an issue. So, I don't think it's the number of people you put into a task. It is how people get the task accomplished.

Concerns about representation reported in the 1997 member-to-member survey decreased from 31 percent before the election of crew coordinators to 19 percent. Still, it ranked as the second-most-commented-on issue. Most comments continued to call for more contact with the elected union leadership, whereas just 5 percent called for electing module advisors.

The local has repeatedly experimented with ways to structure the roles and responsibilities of its senior leadership. It first experimented with rotating its vice presidents among the different business units, partnering them with plant managers, in an attempt to develop leaders with a broad grasp of the business across the company. The local later realigned its resources in response to membership calls for more representation by elected leaders, assigning these vice presidents to servicing assignments by three crews across the site. Executive board members then took on operations' management leadership in each business unit. Responsibilities were reorganized again in 1995, after the contractual change that provided for the election of crew coordinators. Elected vice presidents were once again partnered with the plant managers in each business unit, focusing on co-managing the business along with the jointly selected module advisors and functional coordinators. Designing the organizational structure and assigning leaders to these different roles became a key strategic and political task for the local union leaders, which, as we will see, became a source of internal conflict and tension within the local.

Another major reorganization occurred in February 1996, when Bennett resigned his position as president but retained his role as union MAC advisor. The first vice president, Joe Rypkowski, took over the presidency, creating for the first time the type of dual leadership seen in other UAW locals, in which power is split between the president and the chairperson of the grievance committee. The MAC advisor has authority over the elected crew coordinators, as the chairperson does in a traditional plant. This restructuring of the union organization reflected some recognition of the concerns over individual representation and was an effort to provide a better balance between a participatory and a representative form of union democracy.

Tensions with the National Union

Over the years, the union's practices and structures at Saturn have stirred considerable tension and conflict between local and national UAW leaders. Some of these tensions were inevitable and a natural part of the debates over how to reconcile local and national union interests and responsibilities. The international union clearly has an ongoing interest in maintaining the industrywide standards that it has struggled to achieve over the last fifty years. Saturn departs from a number of long-standing principles and provisions built into the national contract. Seniority rights, job classifications, grievance committee structures, overtime, and compensation plans are all areas in which the Saturn model does not follow the national pattern. From the international's viewpoint, these are deviations from national patterns that might lead to whipsawing (i.e., playing one local off against another) and the undermining of its bargaining power in the industry. Therefore, it is reasonable for the international union to be cautious in embracing a new set of policies that depart from those in place in almost every other plant. Yet these local-national debates over how to adapt to different local needs without eroding national standards are not unique to Saturn but are a growing part of most local-national union interactions. Increasingly, plant-by-plant variations occur as local union leaders and managers adjust practices to achieve greater flexibility, experiment or incorporate different team-based work organization arrangements, and make the case for attracting new technological investments and product placements.

Furthermore, Saturn represents innovation in a greenfield (new) setting. Although all UAW members transferred from other GM locations,
they were still hired into and accepted a new work system within the
new organizational and governance structure. Although these practices
may work well as a complete package in a greenfield, a question remains
about their applicability in an ongoing operation, in which employees
might perceive the change process as an erosion of standards and a loss
of their hard-won rights. To the extent that incumbent workers and members have equity built up in these standards, they would likely oppose
new practices in their plants. Thus, a clear reason for ambivalence on the
part of the international union is an effort to protect and maintain
national standards, built-up equities, and pattern bargaining.

The more that locals negotiate variations from the national contract,
the more power shifts from the national to local leaders. Thus, alongside
debates over the substantive merits of different practices lie issues of
power and control. Over the years in the UAW and in most industrial
unions that negotiated national agreements with large companies,
power gradually shifted from the local to the national level. Now that
trend may be reversing, adding further strain to local-national relations.

Not surprisingly, intertwined with conflicts over these structural and
political power issues have been interpersonal conflicts between key
local and national leaders. We discuss these intertwined conflicts in
some depth here because they not only have had a significant effect on
internal union dynamics, but they inevitably spill over and affect partnership processes and outcomes as well. We do not believe these conflicts are unique to the personalities or political relationships between
this local and international union. Instead, we see them as generic issues
that other local and national union leaders need to manage.

In May 1993, Steve Yokich, then UAW vice president of the GM
department and now UAW president, wrote to Saturn management and
stated his intent to modify the Memorandum of Agreement, Saturn's
contract. The UAW International's effort to modify the Saturn agreement continued until December 1994. Local union leaders interpreted
this as an attempt by the UAW International to pull Saturn back under
the national pattern (also during 1993, a new GM/UAW national agreement was negotiated that called for a union-initiated feasibility study for
a new small car, specifically not to be built by Saturn). The UAW International made proposals to change Saturn's team-hiring responsibility,
make transfers based on seniority, elect crew coordinators, and work

five-day, eight-hour shifts. Also included was a proposal that made the ability to modify the contract the exclusive right of the UAW International rather than the local union. These proposals were rejected by the membership 75 percent to 25 percent and 60 percent to 40 percent in votes held in November and December 1994. After the second vote, the local union president and vice presidents were brought into the negotiations. A new agreement was developed, with two significant changes to the original contract: the election of crew coordinators and the removal of the local union's authority to initiate modifications of the agreement without getting prior approval from the national union. The membership ratification vote took place in late December when one of the three crews was already on vacation. With 70 percent of the membership voting, the agreement was passed 54 percent to 46 percent.

During 1994, when GM was deciding on whether to support Saturn's request for capital to expand production at Spring Hill and design a new model to replace the original, UAW International leaders argued against expanding the Spring Hill facility and favored an alternative proposal to build vehicles under the Saturn nameplate in the Wilmington plant, which was being considered for closure. Exacerbating these natural tensions between local and international leaders was a strong and sometimes public interpersonal conflict between Bennett and Yokich. For example, in 1992, while UAW members were on strike at GM's Lordstown, Ohio, plant, Bennett was quoted in the *Wall Street Journal*:

> The effects of the strike by GM workers at Lordstown continues to cascade through the world's biggest company. The number of idled plants has grown daily, including the Tennessee factory that makes the hugely popular new line of Saturn automobiles. Steve Yokich, the head of the union's GM department, apparently concocts his strategy without a lot of annoying input from the field. If he had consulted with Michael Bennett, head of the UAW's Local 1853 at Saturn, he might have thought twice. "I don't support the current process. We can't continue to remove wages from competition in the international economy," Mr. Bennett told us from Tennessee yesterday. "That's my position, not the UAW position."[6]

This type of public debate made what we see as the more natural or generic tensions between these two levels of the union more difficult to manage or resolve.

The new local union leaders elected in 1999 are determined not to let similar interpersonal conflicts develop with national leaders, and the same determination was voiced to us by Richard Shoemaker, the UAW vice president in charge of the GM department. Thus, this aspect of the local-international dynamics should not interfere with management of the more natural tensions in this relationship.

Local Union Internal Politics

Historically, the sustainability of efforts at labor participation in managerial decision making has been tested by internal political challenges to union leadership. Indeed, the need to be responsive to the membership is one of the democratic checks that help to ensure that union participation does not deteriorate into simple co-optation and lack of responsiveness to rank-and-file concerns. True to this tradition, there has been an active internal political process within the local union at Saturn. Caucuses have arisen as in other UAW local unions. In the 1993 local elections, three new dissident caucuses (the Mission Team, the Clear Vision Team, and the Members for a Democratic Union) challenged the incumbents (the Vision Team). Issues of contention included the electing versus selecting of union partners, rotating versus fixed work schedules, overtime and shift premiums, adequate representation on the floor, and the relationship to the international union. To some extent, these opposition caucuses reflected differences between those members who voluntarily left GM jobs to come to Saturn in the first wave of hiring and those who came in the second or third wave from layoffs or plant closings. Most of the leaders of these opposition caucuses, however, came to Saturn in the first wave of hiring, which makes analyzing the internal politics of the local more complicated than simply relating attitudes to hiring time frames.

Active politics continued after the 1993 election, with the caucuses joining a 1994 debate over whether Saturn should seek needed capital from sources other than GM. Concern over GM's delay in providing additional capital for expanding capacity and new model development resulted in an unprecedented proposal by the incumbent leadership. In an April 1994 newsletter to the membership, Bennett wrote,

> Now, some within General Motors and the UAW are not sure what to do with your success story. They can't live with the success and they can't live without it, especially if Saturn's failure lays at their own doorstep.

One way to kill Saturn, without being indicted, is to cut off the organizational life blood supply of capital. Without adequate capital, Saturn will slowly die. With capital, Saturn would have already had a right hand drive for export. With capital, Saturn would have new models and platforms. With capital, Saturn would have additional manufacturing capability to build and sell 500,000 plus units annually. . . . The best way to predict our future is to create it, and create it we MUST. Saturn's success belongs to you, and if you have an interest in creating your own future, then maybe we need to consider innovative ways of doing just that. If General Motors doesn't have the capital we need or want to provide it, then maybe we could find other investors in America who are interested in our future. Maybe you, the Membership, are interested in becoming owners of Saturn. Maybe our retailers and suppliers are interested in becoming real owners of the business. Maybe General Motors would be interested in selling Saturn to the people who made her a success if they don't know what to do with her.

A proposal to have the local union study alternatives for obtaining needed capital was presented in the May 1994 monthly union meeting that we attended. A floor vote was taken on the question of whether to hold a membership referendum that would authorize the bargaining committee to research new opportunities for capital investment and discuss these with GM. The referendum received the overwhelming support of those present, with only three dissenting votes out of approximately three hundred. The membershipwide referendum scheduled for June 1994 was the subject of fierce political fighting by competing caucuses within the local union. Rumors circulated that Bennett was already negotiating the sale of Saturn to a Japanese automaker. The proposal to authorize the study of alternative sources of capital was a complicated and unfamiliar concept to most of the membership. Many saw it as an immediate step toward separating from the deep pockets of GM, on which they had relied for their entire careers. After vigorous campaigning, the proposal was defeated with 42 percent voting to support such a study and 58 percent against.

Furthermore, the 1996 elections were hotly contested, with Bennett, the incumbent president and MAC advisor, resigning as president two months before the election, which allowed vice president Rypkowski to seek the presidency as an incumbent. When he resigned as president, Bennett retained his position as MAC advisor with responsibility to approve joint appointments and lead the elected crew coordinators. Bennett and Rypkowski were re-elected by sizable margins.

The 1999 elections resulted in the defeat of Bennett and the Vision caucus. Interviews with outgoing as well as newly elected leaders and with rank-and-file union members indicate several factors that appear to have affected the vote to change union leadership:

1. The widely held view that it was time for a change. After thirteen years under the same union administration, members indicated that they were interested in seeing some new faces.
2. The view that the Vision Team had acquired too much power through its ability to approve the selection of the 400 full-time union positions within the partnership structure. Some members worried that politics, not skills and abilities, were becoming more important in the selection process. Although Jeep Williams, the newly elected MAC advisor, raised the possibility of electing module advisors, he told us that he did not think (based on union referendums) that he would get enough support from the rank and file to make that change: "I want to change how module advisors are selected. I would like election for them all, but I don't think that will happen. I want team member involvement in deciding who the candidates will be."
3. The perception by members and some leaders that the local leadership was not adequately balancing individual member representation with the time and resources it was putting into running the business. The issue of balance between collective and individual representation has been a source of debate within the local for many years.

In addition to these three general issues, many specific complaints engaged segments of the electorate. These included ongoing opposition to the shift rotation schedule and a number of concerns precipitated by the softening of the small-car market: reduction of overtime, need to rebalance the assembly line, work force reductions required by the reduced volume, erosion of the risk-and-reward bonuses, and general job insecurity caused by lack of new product as well as downturn in demand. Finally, the opposition caucus appeared to run a more effective campaign. Although the incumbents expected credit for negotiating the possibility of a SUV and the favorable resolution of a disputed bonus for 1998, they were criticized by the opposition for not getting a new product earlier and for the decline in the bonus payout.

Political challenges such as these are a normal part of the democratic process. To date, contrary to the impression encouraged by the popular business press, no caucus has advocated the dismantling of the partnership. Rather, each caucus has advocated its own approach to managing the union's role. The real question is how to manage this democratic process without it spilling over in ways that negatively affect the partnership process and organizational performance. A test of this occurred with the contract negotiations held in the fall of 1999 with Saturn management, the new local leaders, and the international union, which produced an agreement preserving the basic principles of the original Saturn memorandum. Changes included reducing the risk portion of compensation, adding six new elected positions, securing floor input in the selection of module advisors, and wage increases and improvements to pensions and disability benefits to keep Saturn employees in line with other GM employees. The partnership structures were not changed, and Saturn remained independent of the national agreement between the UAW and GM. So, although the Spring Hill local has moved into its next generation of political leadership, the Memo and partnership arrangements have demonstrated staying power and appear to be embedded in the organizational culture of both the company and union.

Conclusion

Just as Saturn has become a symbol for a "Different Kind of Company," in response, UAW Local 1853 has become a "Different Kind of Union." Although many of the features of the Saturn partnership and the local union are unique, they highlight the generic challenges and potential responses of a union engaged in a relationship in which critical decisions affecting worker interests have moved from the bargaining table to the strategic levels of corporate decision making and both worker preferences and production strategies call for direct worker and union participation in workplace processes. Evidence from the Saturn experience suggests a new model of unionism for locals attempting to jointly manage and govern organizations while maintaining their ability to effectively represent their members. Having watched this local union evolve through its first generation, we can identify the critical features of this new model.

1. The capacity to add value to the management and performance of the business by improving both the quality of decision making and the effectiveness of implementation.
2. The ability to represent the collective interests of its members in managerial decision making.
3. The capacity to balance collective representation effectively with representation of individual members whose rights have been violated.
4. The ability and willingness to mobilize the membership and use the leverage it acquires through co-management to sustain the partnership, build the union, and if necessary, confront management in collective bargaining when the parties are in conflict over vital issues.
5. The ability to promote and sustain internal union democracy while managing internal union conflicts in ways that do not limit the sustainability of the partnership.
6. The ability to successfully manage its organizational boundaries, including those with its national union, the corporation, other locals, suppliers, customers, and the community.

Adding Value

It is clear from interviews, observations, and empirical data that in its formative years (from 1985 to about 1993) this local union focused its time, energy, resources, and attention on organizing an institutional role in the governance and management of Saturn. With the onset of production, the local has added value through the substantive knowledge it brings to bear on joint decision making. Through co-management and a dense communications network the local has helped produce quality results.

Representing Worker Interests in Management Decision Making

Although union leaders need to add value to the firm through their roles in the governance or management process, if this is all they do, they are no different from other competent managers. Union leaders must also bring worker interests to bear in the strategic choices and decisions made in these processes. Moreover, this role must be visible and widely communicated and understood by the members so they see the value to them of this form of representation. This can be seen in the union's ability to renegotiate the risk-and-reward formula to reflect market changes and to bring new products into the facility, enhancing the long-term job security of its members while sustaining its role in business decision making.

Representing Individual Rights and Concerns

The focus on direct collective participation, in the eyes of many members, occurred at the expense of individual membership representation. The union then took steps to correct this problem by electing a set of leaders to focus on representing individual member concerns and, if necessary, file grievances.

Yet, even with their concerns for stronger individual representation, the majority of the membership continues to indicate a preference for the Saturn partnership over the option of returning to the traditional GM-UAW system of shop floor relations. They seem to be calling for an alternative that maintains a direct union voice in collective decisions affecting the enterprise and provides worker input into day-to-day operations that affect product quality and the way work is done. They also appear to value the flexibility Saturn and the UAW have shown to ensure employment security when crisis or unanticipated problems arise, such as the alternatives found to temporary shutdowns. At the same time, they want a means for individual advocacy and have chosen to elect those who represent them in this capacity. In short, they seem to want both direct participation in decisions that affect the common goals of the enterprise and an independent voice to represent their individual interests and concerns in the day-to-day implementation and management of the organization. The challenge for unions engaged in partnerships, therefore, is to find an appropriate balance between their role as a representative and their role as a strategic partner with management. Both appear to be essential to the sustainability of a labor-management partnership, and workers want their union to play both roles.

Maintaining Union Power

As in traditional labor management relations, a union will continue to be a viable representative of members' interests only if it is able to mobilize power when it finds workers' vital interests in conflict with an employer's.

In strikes over issues of outsourcing at selected plants in 1992 and 1998, international union leaders demonstrated their ability to exert pressure on GM through strategic use of the strike threat. In this way, they can play a unique role, influencing policies such as sourcing, contracting out, and employment or income guarantees. Through their ability to coordinate action, they can also provide some protection against whipsawing.

On the other hand, the local union at Saturn found new sources of power in its relations with management, both local and corporate, through the acquisition of essential skills and information, the development of managerial competency among local leaders, and the local's ability to internally organize and mobilize human resources. This power can then be exercised both through traditional tactics such as strike threats, and also by challenging the positions taken by management that are believed to be against the long-term interests of the membership and perhaps of other stakeholders as well. This power, evidenced continually by the local, has been increasingly recognized as being critical to the successful operation of fragile, lean, high-performance work organizations. The very nature of these joint governance systems, which are based on the problem solving and decision making competency of the local work force and union leadership, may require that they be created locally.

Local institutional arrangements and the flexibility to adjust rapidly to changing competitive environments may be critical to the survival of contemporary manufacturing organizations. It may no longer be possible to take wages out of competition in global markets. Therefore, unions must both respond directly to the interests of their members and generate power locally to protect those interests.

Managing Union Politics

The intensity of internal union political battles and local-national union conflicts weakens support for the partnership model within both the union and the corporation. Yet union democracy is just as critical to this type of union as to traditional unions. Managing the politics of the local union remains a significant challenge facing these union leaders. Local union leaders at Saturn have attempted to manage internal politics by maximizing rank-and-file input through the widespread use of member-to-member surveys to establish union priorities and membership referendums to make key policy decisions. In addition, several off-site planning sessions aimed at creating unity among competing caucuses were conducted over the years and as recently as 1998.

Managing External Boundaries

The features of union partnership incorporated into the original organizational design and the one that has evolved at Saturn reflect both the historical legacy of the New Deal industrial relations system and the history of union-management relations between the UAW and GM. Furthermore, Saturn illustrates the tensions produced in union structures by implementing stakeholder models. On the one hand, employees are more heavily invested in the future of the firm, and thus some American adaptation of enterprise unions would seem to be a better match than national or international unions. On the other hand, enterprise unions, standing alone, are not able to withstand pressures to compete by driving down wages and other labor standards in the industry, nor are they able to provide political, financial, and expert resources needed to sustain this model in a relatively skeptical or hostile environment. Moreover, the legacy of company unionism in the United States before the passage of the New Deal labor law and the continued strength of anti-unionism within the contemporary American management culture make it difficult to find ways to experiment with an independent local or enterprise body in the United States.

Furthermore, the international union's support is critical to a local union. This was true when Saturn was created, and the fact of it resurfaced at several points when key decisions controlled by GM were being made. The international union's support for the Saturn local has varied over time. At the early stages of development, the international union and GM led the effort by creating the joint study team and by developing the organizing principles articulated in the 1985 Memorandum of Agreement, which provided enabling language. Without this response by the UAW to GM's request to explore new contractual arrangements for small-car production, Saturn would never have been created. The enabling language and guiding principles allowed the parties, both union and management, to move beyond the boundaries of traditional agreements and organizational arrangements. In later years full-time international staff representation was withdrawn and replaced only when efforts to modify the contract were under way.

The international made efforts to bring the local back under the national agreement, and it has witheld support for new products and capacity expansion. It also withdrew its participation on the SAC from 1991 until 1995, leaving union participation in that organization to the local.

This raises additional questions regarding the appropriate relationship between the local and the international union. What support, resources, and guidance from the international continue to be needed? How can the equities built up by members in existing plants be protected if they adopt some of Saturn's practices? How are the policies and practices of one local to be coordinated with those of other local unions? To be effective, how much independence does a local union such as Saturn's require in its negotiations and institutional arrangements, and to what extent can it be expected to adhere to broader national policies and concerns for solidarity? Resolving these substantive and highly political issues is a critical challenge and requirement for unions engaged in partnership arrangements. In the long run, the performance of the local union will depend on local and international leaders' working together to find the right mix of local autonomy, international leadership support, and mutual organizational learning.

If we can, in fact, generalize from the Saturn case in the ways suggested here, local unions engaged in partnership models will need to balance these different and partially conflicting pressures and requirements. Maximizing any one of these features is likely to lead to problems. For example, by assuming complete authority to negotiate its own contract without regard to national union standards the local risks losing the support it will need from national union leaders when decisions critical to member interests are made at levels beyond the local's control. Focusing solely on participation in governance processes and decisions will likely lead to a membership backlash in which members demand more effective individual representation, as they did at Saturn. Too little attention to internal union democracy will likely produce a rival or dissident faction that challenges incumbent union leaders. Too much internal political conflict may frustrate management partners and limit the ability or willingness of union leaders to accept responsibility and accountability for decisions made in joint processes. Thus, *balance* across these features may be the critical requirement.

5

Boundary Management and Learning Disabilities

 n a 1992 article, *Business Week* called attention to GM's dilemma over what to do with Saturn.

> Saturn's sudden blast up the sales charts is heartening for its troubled parent. . . . As foreign rivals continue to flood the market with new models, Saturn is meeting these head-on. Almost overnight, Saturn has become the highest quality American-made brand, with as few defects as Hondas and Nissans. It's stunningly successful at satisfying the customer, trailing only Lexus and Infiniti, according to researcher J. D. Power & Associates.
>
> So the automaker clearly has a winner on its hands. Now the question is: Will GM know what to do with it?[1]

In 1997 another *Business Week* article noted that in the intervening years GM apparently had not been able to decide what to do with Saturn.

> In its zeal to save older brands, GM has ignored what may be its best opportunity for winning younger buyers. When its Saturn division premiered in 1990, it captured boomers with its upstart, anti-Detroit image. But after seven years, Saturn still offers only a modestly restyled version of its original subcompact, leaving nothing for early buyers to trade up to. "If GM took all the money it put into Oldsmobile and spent it on Saturn, they could have created a Saturn minivan and sport-utility that would have sold like crazy," says John Wolkonowicz [head of GM's Oldsmobile divison]. "And Saturn would probably be the No. 1 American automotive division today." GM doesn't deny the gaffe. "There are a

lot of calls we didn't make right. You can just add [Saturn] to the list,"
says GM's [Richard] Wagoner.[2]

The magazine captured the most important and long-lasting controversy confronting Saturn and GM—a conflict that went unresolved so
long that some critics believe the ultimate decision may have come too
late. Why didn't GM continue to support the evolution of Saturn from its
initial product into a broader family of vehicles that could build on its
initial loyal customer base? From the vantage point of employees and
managers at Spring Hill, Tennessee, the answer is simply the myopic
view of GM—executives were unwilling to make the hard choices of
scaling down or closing an existing division such as Oldsmobile, Buick,
Pontiac, or Chevrolet to give Saturn the capital resources and new products needed for it to grow in a timely fashion. From Detroit's perspective, it is the Spring Hill advocates who are myopic: How could GM
justify more resources for Spring Hill and Saturn in the early to mid-
1990s, when all other divisions were starved for new products and the
company was trying to reintegrate and rationalize design and engineering groups, centralize sourcing decisions, and reduce the number of
overlapping product lines while it had excess manufacturing capacity
within existing plants?

In this chapter, we trace the history of this controversy from the first
time requests were made for additional capacity in Spring Hill to the
decision that came out of the negotiations of 1998 to build a SUV in
Spring Hill for marketplace entry in 2001. We use this issue to illustrate
two broader problems that Saturn and its parent organizations experienced over its first generation: (1) difficulties in managing what we refer
to as *boundary relationships*—particularly relations among GM, national
UAW leaders, and their counterparts in Spring Hill, and (2) difficulties in
learning across these boundaries.

These are both generic problems for new organizations; in some ways,
greenfield sites always have what others have called a "liability of new-
ness"[3]—that is, new organizations set up to test and demonstrate the
value of an alternative approach often become isolated from the parent
organization, and the parties have difficulty transferring the lessons from
the new experiences to other parts of the organization.[4] In turn, by giving
the new entity its own space (i.e., the greenfield) to experiment with new
practices, a culture tends to build within the new entity that "we're different and have little or nothing to learn from the rest of the organization."

The problems Saturn, GM, and the UAW experienced with this generic learning disability are taken up in the second half of this chapter.

Initial Plan

The initial plan approved by the GM board for Saturn called for an investment of $5 billion and a vehicle capacity of 500,000 vehicles per year. Before the facility was built, however, the investment was scaled back to $3 billion and the maximum capacity to 330,000. The initial facility was therefore built to provide capacity for Saturn's first model, although the business plan still anticipated that the additional capacity would be necessary for Saturn to realize its financial objectives and sales projections.

Endless Debate: Wither Mod II

As early as 1992, there was an active debate within Saturn, GM, and the UAW International union over the future product stream for Saturn. By this time, Saturn's original champions were gone. Al Warren and Roger Smith had retired from GM, and Don Ephlin had retired from the UAW. Given the lead times required to bring a new model to the market, 1992 may have been about the optimal time to make these decisions and begin the development process. But this was not to be, in part because GM was in deep financial trouble in 1992. It lost $4.5 billion that year! As a result, cost reduction became the critical issue for the corporation and for Saturn. Pressures were put on Saturn by GM President Lloyd Reuss to reduce costs and become profitable that year, two years ahead of the original business plan.

Given these pressures, Saturn president Skip LeFauve reported to the Strategic Action Council that any discussion of Mod II (Module II, the next-generation product they hoped would be authorized for Saturn and brought to the market in 1995) was out of the question until Saturn could get its costs down and become profitable and GM could staunch the corporatewide losses. It was clear to all that the jobs of GM President Reuss and chief executive officer Robert Stempel were on the line. Thus, at a June 1992 meeting, the SAC was informed that product programs planned for 1995, 1996, and 1997 all had to be moved back, perhaps two to three years, at Saturn and in other GM divisions.

The issue of Mod II came up repeatedly in SAC meetings throughout 1993. In April it was noted that GM's North American Operations (NAO) strategy board was discussing Saturn's proposal for Mod II but that it wanted to discuss the plan with UAW President Steve Yokich before taking it to GM's Board of Directors. A series of meetings was held by various Saturn and GM executives with Yokich. The message from the UAW President was clear and consistent: He opposed any plan for Mod II in Spring Hill. Any plan for Mod II, wherever produced, would have to be done under the national UAW-GM contract. The 1993 National Agreement actually contained language providing for a new small car, specifically not to be a Saturn.

Given the difficulty in getting new capital authorized from GM, the option of raising funds from other sources was quietly being discussed at Saturn. At one point, it was reported that GE Capital was willing to invest. In early 1994, Mike Bennett, local union president of UAW Local 1853, publicly raised the question of getting outside investors or implementing an employee stock ownership plan (ESOP) to raise funds for new products and give Saturn employees greater control over their own destiny. After a two-month internal debate, the local union rejected the proposal to study ways of raising outside capital for Saturn.

GM executives also rejected the idea of allowing Saturn to seek alternative sources of capital, indicating that it would be unfair to GM shareholders to introduce outside investors or an ESOP. As GM's Chief Executive Wagoner reflected on this issue in a 1999 interview, "Since GM had put up such a big initial investment, GM shareholders should get the full returns." Both the ESOP and the outside investor ideas were therefore discarded.

By mid-1994 discussions of plans for Mod II were intertwined with debates over how Saturn fit within the evolving GM strategy and structure. During this period, GM was first considering and then announced a major restructuring of its divisions aimed at integrating its different platforms and engineering groups. In September the new structure was described to SAC members. Saturn would become part of GM's new Small Car Group. A week after this decision was reported to the SAC, LeFauve was appointed head of the GM Small Car Group. Although this meant he would leave his post as Saturn's president, he indicated that it bode well for Saturn: "If I thought Saturn was getting swallowed, then I would have fought harder. The alternative was I could stay at Saturn and have someone else take on Small Car—that would ensure that Saturn would be swallowed, for sure."

But the debate over whether Saturn would get authorization for a second model, and what that model would be, continued. Yokich's opposition to expanding Spring Hill continued to be a major factor in the debate and ultimate decision. Referring to a conversation with Yokich, LeFauve reported in July 1995, "His words with me [were] 'We can build quality cars low cost under the national agreement,' and [he] wants to prove that."[5] The use of several other existing GM plants came under consideration as alternatives to expanding Spring Hill. One was GM's Willow Run, Michigan, plant that was scheduled to close. Another option was to use the excess capacity available in GM's Corvette plant in Bowling Green, Kentucky, because it was only a hundred miles up Interstate 65 from Spring Hill, but that idea was also opposed by Yokich. A third alternative was GM's Wilmington, Delaware, plant.[6]

The Wilmington plant had been assembling the Chevrolet Corsica and Berretta lines, both of which were scheduled to be phased out. Wilmington would close down if no new product was brought into the plant, and, indeed, in 1992 GM announced its intention to close Wilmington by 1996. The local union and management at Wilmington looked for ways to save the plant. They studied NUMMI and other lean production systems and tried to leverage their reputation within GM for quality and efficiency. In 1994 the local parties drafted new contract language under the national agreement that called for team-based production, cross-training, job rotation, craft combinations, the replacement of supervisors with production coordinators, and joint union-management governance committees to guide the new production system. In 1995—even without plans for a product—85 percent of the members ratified the new agreement. When he learned of the possibility of a Saturn being assembled outside of Spring Hill, Tennessee, Delaware Governor Tom Carper appealed to GM executives to bring the new product to Wilmington. Over the course of 1994 and 1995, the discussion narrowed to the Wilmington and Spring Hill options.

Finally, in 1995, GM and the UAW negotiated an agreement to keep Wilmington open. The plan was to assemble a new product temporarily called the Innovate that would be designed by GM's German subsidiary, Opel. In August 1996 GM announced that the Innovate would be the next-generation Saturn model, now called the LS (large Saturn.) The Mod II decision was made four years after discussions had begun and a year after Saturn's initial plan called for its second-generation vehicle to be ready for sale. The plan called for the Innovate to be delivered in model year 1999. Later the date was changed to model year 2000.

LeFauve said that the partnership agreement operating in Spring Hill would remain intact; he also stated his belief that the same cooperative spirit and results achieved in Spring Hill could be achieved in Wilmington under the GM-UAW national agreement. But then, the local president and shop chairperson at Wilmington, who led the effort for a new local agreement in 1994, were defeated in the 1996 elections. The new leaders ran against the team concept, and while the new local president, Joe Brennan, stated his willingness to engage in a partnership with management to produce Saturns under a new team-based work system, the shop chair, Suman Bohm, was opposed to this. Although teams were implemented in Wilmington, the joint-governance arrangements envisioned by the new agreement were not. Instead, as Brennan stated in July 1999, "meetings took place for three years every Monday for one to five hours. The contract and issues from the floor were discussed. It was essentially an extended grievance meeting." In April 1999 Bohm was defeated by Scott Faraday, who took office as shop chair in June. Faraday has expressed strong interest in changing labor-management relations at Wilmington. He has said that he wants to create a partnership and help run the business. As of this writing, it is too early to say how this change of leadership will affect Wilmington's version of the Saturn partnership.

The decision to locate Mod II in Wilmington had significant negative effects on morale at Spring Hill. Not only did the work force and many of the local leaders feel betrayed, but also, the move raised for the first time real fears of job insecurity because it was clear that the base Saturn model was getting old. Without the commitment of some new product for Spring Hill, the employment guarantees in the original Memorandum of Agreement could not be fulfilled. Everyone at Saturn knew this. As Saturn leaders expressed dismay over the expansion of capacity outside Spring Hill, some saw the move as an erosion of GM's commitment to the principles and organizational design of the partnership model. Some also saw it as a betrayal of trust, because they had accomplished everything asked of them and expected the promised second module in return.

By 1998 concern over GM's delay in providing additional capital to Spring Hill for expanded capacity and new model development precipitated two crises. Saturn's risk-and-reward bonus formula is contingent on meeting mutually negotiated goals for quality, cost, schedule, and volume. Although the 1996 reward bonus was $10,000, when the small-car market softened with lower gasoline prices in 1997, it became clear that the bonuses for the last two quarters would be nonexistent (the total

1997 bonus based on performance during the first two quarters was $2,017). The union attempted to renegotiate the risk-and-reward metrics, suggesting an emphasis on cost reduction instead of volume, with the goal of reducing prices to consumers and increasing market share. Local Saturn management resisted the change until the end of the year and finally settled on a new formula in January 1998. After this was announced to the membership, GM corporate executives in Detroit said they could not support the change. This resulted in a vote by the membership to hold a referendum on whether to continue working under the partnership agreement or attempt to adopt the UAW national agreement with GM. After this vote was taken and before the actual referendum, GM agreed to a new risk-and-reward formula for the Saturn local that was based on lower production targets.

Job security, however, continued to be a concern as lower sales volumes continued and no new products were forthcoming at Spring Hill. Furthermore, Saturn's autonomy in decision making had been eroding since October 1994, when it was integrated into GM's small-car group. This loss left local union leaders frustrated. As LeFauve and then several other top-level Saturn executives who had been in place throughout most of its history left Saturn for GM positions or retired (by the end of 1998, the vice presidents of Engineering, People Systems, Finance, and Manufacturing all were gone), the perception built within the work force and among a number of members of the local union executive board in Spring Hill that Saturn's influence in GM had declined considerably.

During the summer of 1998, while a number of other GM local unions were striking against the corporation over outsourcing, the local at Saturn authorized its leadership to call for a strike if concerns about decision making, new products, and risk-and-reward were not resolved. After a month of intense negotiations that included the local and international unions, as well as Saturn and GM management, an agreement was reached on the risk-and-reward formula, decision-making authority, sourcing, and new products. Finally, in April 1999, GM announced its intention (contingent on further analysis of a detailed product portfolio plan for Saturn) to build a new SUV in Spring Hill. This decision would bring capacity up to the original plan of 500,000 vehicles a year and add an additional 1,000 members to the bargaining unit. But the commitment to build a follow-on product in Spring Hill occurred only after the local union had made this the critical issue in crisis negotiations.

Seven years of debate, discussion, and indecision went by before Spring Hill finally got a commitment to build its second-generation product. Still, further uncertainties over the future of the manufacturing operations continue. At the moment, questions have arisen around the Powertrain operations at Saturn, because Saturn's future engines and transmissions will likely come from a common GM platform. Whether some of these powertrains will be sourced in Spring Hill is a matter under discussion. The outcome of those discussions will have an important bearing on the nature of the Spring Hill operations as well as on the number and mix of jobs the location can support. The discussions about resource allocation go on, and this is likely to be a topic of continuous debates that will have an impact on job security, work force morale, and performance. How these decisions are made and communicated, as well as their substantive outcomes, will have major effects on the future of the partnership and therefore on Saturn.

Efforts to Learn—General Motors, the United Auto Workers, and External Visitors

One of Saturn's stated objectives was to serve as a laboratory for experimentation and learning for the corporation. During the creation and early development of Saturn, Roger Smith, GM's CEO, stated its goal as "improving the efficiency and competitiveness of every plant we operate. . . . Saturn is the key to GM's long-term competitiveness, survival, and success as a domestic producer."[7]

The transfer of lessons learned at Saturn proved to be much more difficult than anticipated, however. To illustrate this, in 1995 we briefed a group of senior GM executives on the results of our study of the impact of the partnership on quality and discussed how others in the company might learn from these data. One executive said, "It's ironic but unfortunately true that Ford has written a better report on Saturn and learned more from it than has anyone in GM." Another asked, "Is there some way you can present these data in a more generic form so that our managers won't know they are from Saturn? Once they know you're talking about Saturn, they'll just tune you out and say, 'They're different'."

The barriers to learning were just as strong, if not stronger, on the union side as in GM. In 1996, we held two workshops with Saturn union and management leaders at Rutgers University. The Rutgers campus is an hour and a half drive up Interstate 95 from the Wilmington plant. It seemed logical to us that this was a venue for breaking the ice between the union and management peers in the two facilities. So we asked the Spring Hill participants if they would like to build a meeting with their Wilmington counterparts into the session. They readily agreed that this would be a good idea. We raised the subject with union and management leaders in Wilmington, making it clear that our intent was to arrange a *social* opportunity to meet with their counterparts, not to engage in a substantive analysis or discussion of what practices and experiences in Spring Hill might mean for Wilmington. We even said that the invitation would come from John Burton, the Rutgers dean, who was hosting the session, so that it would not appear that we were trying to brainwash or proselytize about the partnership. Burton would invite a group from Wilmington to join the Spring Hill group for an informal dinner. Even this level of dialogue was not to be, however. Word came from Wilmington that, given the political sensitivities of Detroit (i.e., the UAW national leaders), it would not be possible to accept the invitation from us or from the dean. The dinner never happened, even though leaders from Spring Hill were essentially meeting in Wilmington's backyard.

These experiences reinforce the public perception that GM and the UAW have failed to learn from their experiences at Saturn. By and large, we agree with this general perception. Indeed, in our discussions with GM and UAW national leaders, we have been surprised by their lack of understanding of how Saturn actually operates. More than once, for example, eyebrows were raised when we described the extensive system of co-management that lies at the heart of Saturn's operations. Most of what GM and UAW leaders know and think about Saturn has been derived from secondary reports rather than from direct personal contacts.

The picture is not quite as bleak as it may appear, however. Some of Saturn's features have caught the attention of others at GM, and there now appears to be a growing understanding of what could be learned from Saturn if appropriate efforts were made. For example, Saab executives worked closely with Saturn to learn about its marketing approach. In fact, the experience of both NUMMI and Saturn has been that GM's European division has been quicker to adopt ideas from these two operations than have GM's North American counterparts. GM's new plants in Eisenach, Germany, as well as several others in Poland, Brazil, Argentina, and China, are being modeled after NUMMI with the help of a team of managers who led the NUMMI effort.[8]

Saturn's retail strategies have been acknowledged to be the best in the corporation, and some are being used in a number of other divisions, particularly by the Oldsmobile organization. Transfers of several key Saturn executives to the GM parent organization has also led to some diffusion of Saturn's engineering and technical innovations. Jay Wetzel, the head of Saturn's Engineering, was promoted to vice president for engineering for all of GM's NAO. He carried over many of the processes and principles developed at Saturn to NAO's engineering and product development processes.

Some within GM have also visited Saturn to learn from its experiences. Too often, they failed to focus on those unique core aspects of Saturn that made it higher performing than other parts of GM. Table 5-1 uses survey data to compare what visitors from GM divisions choose to focus on with the choices of visitors from other organizations. The data cover visits

Table 5-1. What Visitors from General Motors Divisions Focus on Compared with Visitors from Other Organizations

Topics	Other Organizations (%)	General Motors (%)
Self-managed teams	15	9
Cultural change/empowerment	14	3
Training	10	7
Union/management partnership	9	6
Supplier relations overview	8	3
EXCEL (all phases)	8	48
Customer enthusiasm	7	1
People development	6	5
Quality overview	4	3
Compensation: risk-and-reward	3	0
Team-building methods/techniques	3	1
Consultation process	2	3
Internal communications	2	3
Just-in-time inventory/material flow	2	1
Safety/ergonomics	2	2
Electronic Data Systems—technical overview and supplier relations	1	0
Human resources overview	1	1
Maintenance overview/total preventive	1	0
Manufacturing process	1	1
Marketing approach	1	0
Assistance center overview	0	0
Experiential learning activity	0	0
Visits	1,383	82

Source: Saturn Consulting Services.

made between 1995 and 1999 and were collected by Saturn's Consulting Services, a department within Saturn that hosts visitors and provides training and consulting to outside organizations. Of 1,465 visits, GM accounted for only 82 (5.6 percent). Furthermore, although non-GM visitors came to learn about a broad range of topics (self-managed teams, 15 percent; cultural change/empowerment, 14 percent; training, 10 percent; union-management partnership, 9 percent; supplier relations, 8 percent; Saturn's EXCEL four-phase team-building course, 8 percent), nearly half the GM visitors focused on the EXCEL course (48 percent).

These GM visitors are a little like the poor guy looking for his lost keys under the light post. The keys are not likely to be found there, but it is the only place one can safely look without stumbling in the darkness. In the case of the GM visitors, to look more intensively at the different components of the partnership—team-based work systems, co-management, representational structures such as the MAC, and so forth—would risk stumbling into organizational design and labor-management issues outside their control and unacceptable within the prevailing GM-UAW culture.

The Deeper Lessons of Saturn

What lessons should different parties take away from the Saturn experience? Saturn leaders took up this issue in a special SAC meeting held in April 1996. The participants asked themselves, "What 'value' does Saturn provide to GM?" They produced two lists, summarized in Table 5-2: the criteria they believe GM should focus on and see in assessing their success, and the "critical success factors" that they believe produce these results. One participant summed up these factors, commenting that the " advantage Saturn has is the degree of integration it has with retailers, suppliers, the UAW, and its [other] parts."

LeFauve made the same point. He stressed that the essence of Saturn is in the trust and quality of the relationships across the different stakeholders, and he is emphatic about the need to see these as a highly interdependent system.

The bottom line is that's what made Saturn what it was. It was involving the people in the factory; it was involving the dealers, involving suppliers. Everybody, when it came to a decision that was going to affect them, [got] some form of representation [who] was again responsible to go

Table 5-2. Self-Assessment: Saturn's Value to General Motors

Success Criteria:
Successful brand
High quality
High customer satisfaction
Reduced customer cost
Profitable
Increased reliability
Critical Factors Contributing to Success:
Partnership
Simultaneous engineering
Integrated systems—social/technical
Dealer agreement/franchise
Production system
Parts systems
Direct report of our people
Ability to identify and solve problems with information

back to them and tell them that "we made the decision, and I participated." But that's the [key to] Saturn.

We also asked a number of other parties this question. Wagoner, GM's CEO, noted in a 1999 inverview that for GM, clearly the most important contribution is the brand image that Saturn has achieved: "Saturn has built a particularly good brand image with customers— that's the key contribution. We need to take advantage of this."

Although like most other GM executives who look at Saturn from the outside, he sees the biggest contribution coming from Saturn's retail successes, he also recognizes that its success in this area is linked to a deeper feature—the quality of the relationships Saturn has built throughout its organization.

> This [retail success] comes from all the pieces of Saturn—its new marketing concept—market areas; no-haggle prices; good relationships among the parts of the organization—factory-dealer; among the workers in the plant, with the union; excellent communications processes; better understanding of the auto business by the work force that makes the business aspects real to them; and high trust relations with suppliers.

This was the first time we heard a GM executive (other than one of the Saturn Alumni) articulate the importance of the rich network of relationships that make up the system at Saturn. This, we believe, is the heart of the lessons that Saturn offers GM, the UAW, and others. For Saturn to be successful, the network must have powerful ties across the different stakeholders and must be built on the dense communications links within and between the different groups that spread information quickly and use information to solve problems as they arise. This ability to mobilize around problems is a source of strength we observed at Saturn repeatedly—the response to the cost pressures in 1992, the recall crisis in 1993, and the highly successful product launch processes in 1996, 1997, and 1999. These network ties provide the means for capitalizing on the singular focus on quality that lies deep in the Saturn philosophy and culture and is embedded in the pride of the work force.

What about from the perspective of the international union? What, if anything is there to learn from Saturn? We think there are several things. First, regardless of whether one agrees with the ideas behind the Saturn partnership, the creation of this organization provided jobs to members either out of work or transferring from plants that were downsizing. It has further increased UAW membership by organizing the amalgamated units and providing work for GM and allied UAW plants. Saturn provides more than 8,300 UAW jobs in Spring Hill, Tennessee, and Troy, Michigan, including the new amalgamated local units. In addition, it has already created an additional 3,500 UAW jobs in existing GM allied-division component plants, 350 UAW jobs in nonallied suppliers, 250 union non-UAW jobs in suppliers, and more than 2,500 nonunion jobs in supplier operations across the United States.

Second, it demonstrates the power to be derived from adding managerial value to the enterprise and being involved in business decisions before they are made. The leverage gained by the local through co-managing business decisions has been evident over the years, most recently in the 1998 negotiations with GM over the risk-and-reward bonuses and over decision-making authority and new products.

Third, it lays bare the multiple roles local union leaders need to play today and the need to find the right balance across these roles to be successful politically. It also raises a question as to the appropriate balance of power between national unions trying to create and maintain standards and locals engaged in co-management that are more knowledgeable about business needs at the enterprise level.

These lessons do not imply that all other parts of GM or the UAW should embrace and adopt Saturn's structures and practices. Indeed, this would not work. Instead, the value of learning about the strengths and weaknesses of these aspects of Saturn's partnership is to engage in discussions within the organizations about whether they would work or how to adapt them to fit into different settings.

Why Is Learning So Hard?

If these indeed are the key lessons, why has it been so hard to see and learn from them? We think there are several factors at work here, most of which are not unique to Saturn but reflect generic difficulties experienced in greenfield sites.[9]

When Saturn was created, its champions specifically set it apart and worked hard to give it the autonomy and space it needed to experiment. As Al Warren, GM's vice president of labor relations at the time, told us,

> I tried to get the corporation and the international [union] to stay as far from it as I could, so it would be away from tradition. . . . We kept it as an island from GM operations people to keep out their influence. There were curiosity and interest from outside, but we shielded it. We wanted it self-sufficient as much as possible. Once under way I stepped away from it. I personally stayed as far from it as I could, so they could run their own show without corporate interference. . . . Part of [the reason] why the ideas did not come across to GM was that we kept the traditional organization away from Saturn.

This made good sense at the time, but what was missed right at the start was the need to think through what mechanisms for learning would be in place once Saturn's original champions retired. Both Warren and Don Ephlin had retired, from GM and the UAW, respectively, before the first Saturn was sold. Smith retired as GM's CEO shortly after he drove the first Saturn off the line in 1990.

The original champions were motivated to learn from Saturn because they both believed in its mission and philosophy and felt ownership of it. With their careers at risk, they each had a personal stake in its success. Their successors did not, in part because they had different views on the power sharing and other features of the partnership, in part because they did not feel the same ownership, and in part because the problems they faced were different and called for different actions and solutions. By the time Saturn was first beginning to experience success in the marketplace, GM was in a deep financial crisis that forced a focus on cost control and delays in capital investment. The UAW was facing further layoffs, plant closings, and outsourcing battles. These short-term crises, along with the lack of any institutional structure or process for learning, reinforced the us-them mentality between participants on the two sides of the Saturn-parent organizational divide.

Then as GM sales rebounded in the mid-1990s, the focus shifted to the hot-selling and higher-margin trucks and SUVs. Commitment to innovation and continuous improvement through workplace reforms declined not just at GM, but at Ford and Chrysler as well. Assembly plant survey data collected by our colleagues, Fritz Pils and John Paul MacDuffie, showed that the rate of diffusion of teams, employee participation, and related human resource practices that supported the lean production system slowed to nearly a halt in U.S. plants in the 1990s.[10]

As far back as 1993, these learning difficulties were visible to anyone looking closely at the Saturn-GM-UAW relationship. We discussed it with Saturn leaders at a SAC meeting in October 1993 and, at their invitation, proposed creating an organizational learning council that would involve union and management leaders at Saturn and GM and perhaps some outside experts. The idea was well received but never implemented.

The problems in learning were not limited to these cross-boundary problems. Although Saturn was created by a benchmarking process that reviewed ongoing innovations at GM and best practices in the industry worldwide, over time Saturn stopped learning from its own experiences as well as from outside sources. For example, in 1992 we discussed with Saturn leaders our observation that they lacked an effective off-line problem-solving process. They agreed, and a workshop was held with a cross-section of union and management leaders at Saturn in which problem-solving processes from Toyota, Honda, Nissan, Xerox, and other leading organizations were discussed. Out of this came a Saturn system for problem solving. Yet, seven years later only approximately 10 percent of the work force is regularly engaged in formal off-line problem solving. In 1993, the productivity and first-time quality levels achieved at Saturn were benchmarked against the data collected by MacDuffie. These data were discussed at a SAC meeting. They showed that Saturn's productivity levels at the time were pretty good relative to the GM average but did not approach the levels achieved in the most productive assembly plants in the United States or abroad. Data on quality showed that although customer satisfaction was world class, first-time quality levels were not very high. This was in part a result of the new manufacturing system that, when introduced, produced a new level of quality but did not include a robust off-line problem-solving process for continuous improvement. In other words, quality was being delivered to retailers and customers because the system emphasized that problems, when they occurred, were to be caught and fixed before the vehicles left the factory, a rather costly approach when compared with a system based on root cause analysis and learning.

Our analysis of what produced quality and, most important, affected the rate of quality improvement showed that the keys lie deep in the co-management process—the richness of communications, the alignment of leaders' views on their tasks, and the balance of people and production issues. These were presented to various groups at Saturn at different times and particularly in three off-site workshops at MIT and Rutgers in 1996 and 1997. Each time, participants agreed that these were critical ingredients in their quality successes, but no action was taken to refocus on the findings and implement changes based on them. In fact, the organization made changes that unintentionally compromised the communications, alignment, and balance of module advisors.

We recite these events here to make the point that there is clearly the potential to learn from Saturn's successes and shortcomings. Learning from their experiences—positive and negative—is essential if the parties at Saturn, in GM, and in the UAW are to address successfully the challenges they face. But the parties have never put in place a proactive process to promote and sustain learning—especially mutual learning. The consequence is that those on the outside see only the superficial visible features of Saturn—the formal partnership structures, cultural training, successful customer relations, and brand image. Those with more specific information also see the quantitative performance measures—the quality, productivity, cost, and profitability numbers. When one of these numbers is good, it is recognized and becomes the focus of attention. This is the case with customer satisfaction and, to a lesser extent, with Saturn's launch performance. When one or more of these numbers is not so good, however, the tendency is to say there is nothing to learn from Saturn. This has been the case in recent years, as Saturn's productivity, cost, and profitability performance declined in response to the aging of its first generation of vehicles and the decline in the small-car market.

For real learning to take place, there must be a willingness to engage in mutual learning, not a one-way transfer from the innovator to the traditional parts of the organization. It must be continuous and linked to changing benchmarks and developments in the external world. It must also be driven by a recognition that all the parties have a strong stake in the success of Saturn—at Spring Hill, Wilmington, and other locations, as well as in GM and the UAW.

These conditions may now be beginning to take hold. Although we focused on the learning disabilities that dominated the first generation, we believe the parties may be about to outgrow them. They will not do so naturally or automatically, however. The first step is to acknowledge them and then take actions to overcome them. If they continue uncorrected, Saturn and its parent organizations will very likely repeat the ups and downs in the second generation they experienced in the first.

What Have We Learned?

The popular press loves to idolize successes, if only to set them up to later report their demise. Saturn is a good case in point. It was the darling of the business press in the mid-1990s. More recently, in the wake of its tough negotiations in 1998 and 1999, the turnover of union leaders, and the slumping demand for its products, many in the press have written off Saturn as another example of failed labor-management cooperation. We hope we have debunked this simplistic view of Saturn as an unmitigated success or failure and the popularly expressed reasons for its various ups and downs. If anything, the conflicts resolved in negotiations in the last several years and the turnover in union leadership have strengthened the partnership by demonstrating that the parties can face difficult issues and survive leadership transitions.

This is not to say that Saturn is not at risk. It does face difficult challenges that need to be addressed to successfully navigate the transition into its second generation. Thus, we will outline what leaders at Saturn, General Motors, and the United Auto Workers need to do if Saturn is to be sustained as a stakeholder, partnership-based organization. What we present here are views we have shared with these leaders, and judging from their reactions to date, views on which they are acting with considerable vigor.

We then turn to the broader implications of this case, recognizing that few labor-management relationships or organizations will take on all the features of Saturn as it was originally designed or as it evolved over the first phase of its organizational life. Instead, we focus on the lessons Saturn offers for those who will be shaping the future of labor-management practices and policies and of organizations that incorporate teams, networks, stakeholder principles, and greater levels of industrial democracy.

Alternative Scenarios

Saturn could conceivably experience any one of three possible scenarios in the years ahead:

1. It could build on its past success and reestablish itself as a highly innovative and successful auto company with new models and a robust labor-management partnership. Perhaps its second-generation models will give it a renewed life in the marketplace, and local labor and management leaders will break down the barriers to learning within GM and the UAW and fulfill Saturn's original mission of being a test track for new practices and relationships.
2. It could fail, especially if it cannot rebound from the declining sales of its base model, if its next-generation models are not well received in the marketplace, or if the new union and management leaders are unable to sustain the partnership.
3. It could sputter along somewhere between these two extremes, by continuing to try to go its own way in Spring Hill, Tennessee, while GM gradually absorbs and centralizes more of Saturn's management functions, the way it manages its other brands and divisions.

If the first scenario plays out, Saturn's success will have a thousand fathers (and at least a few mothers) ready to take credit for its resilience and resurgence. If the second scenario takes place, there will be legions of managers, labor leaders, academics, and others who say, "I told you so." They will claim that Saturn was doomed to fail and simply shows that a company can't be run based on a labor-management partnership or stakeholder model of the firm. And if the third scenario predicts reality, Saturn will fade into the footnotes of organizational and labor relations history—another short-lived experiment that came and went.

Saturn's new leaders are committed to ensuring that the first scenario—resurgence and growth—dictates events and are taking actions to secure these results. GM and national UAW leaders also are beginning to appreciate what's at stake at Saturn and to articulate where it fits into their larger strategies and structures. This provides a basis for optimism and bodes well for Saturn's future. To be successful, however, Saturn's leaders need to adapt its basic principles in ways that address the key problems.

Second-Generation Challenges and Strategies

Saturn embodies many of the features of what theorists have in mind when they envision a stakeholder firm and a networked organization. Indeed, if our analysis is correct, Saturn's key competitive advantage arises out of the brand image and operational responsiveness it has created through the dense network of communications and coordination among its multiple stakeholders.

Nevertheless, Saturn will need to both continue and reinvigorate its labor-management partnership if the company is to survive and prosper. The partnership is a necessary and critical component to the interconnected network of high-trust relationships with its employees, retailers, suppliers, and customers. If the partnership with its employees and union breaks down or returns to a more traditional adversarial or arm's-length pattern, the rest of the principles and values that underlie Saturn's success in relationships with other stakeholders will likewise erode and eliminate this critical source of competitive advantage.

Stakeholder partnerships are fragile arrangements built on trust. They are especially liable to atrophy or break down in periods of leadership transition such as the one Saturn is experiencing. Thus, the issues discussed here should not be viewed as unique to Saturn but instead as generic issues facing an evolving labor-management partnership and stakeholder firm.

Managing Boundary Relations: Saturn, General Motors, and the United Auto Workers

The other issues facing Saturn pale in comparison to the need to better manage the boundary relationships among Saturn, GM, and UAW national leaders. Indeed, this is a central part of the Saturn story. If relations across the GM-UAW-Saturn boundaries are not managed better by all the parties, internal improvements will fall short of what is needed and, in the end, prove to be short-lived.

Saturn and GM have to find a new way to coexist given the more centralized structure and strategy GM is implementing for its models and platforms. GM is attempting to lower costs and rationalize its product portfolio by recentralizing operations and outsourcing more work to suppliers. If Saturn is treated just like all other GM brands, it will experience increasingly strong pressure to outsource components and implement the new modular manufacturing-assembly strategy. But this would conflict with the template for making sourcing decisions agreed to in 1998 contract negotiations. A letter of understanding attached to the 1998 agreement commits Saturn and the UAW to continue making sourcing decisions jointly by balancing concerns for job security, quality, brand equity, and cost. Although Saturn must recognize it is a part of the larger GM strategy and find a way to work within the new GM structure, GM must recognize the need for Saturn to remain sufficiently autonomous to be true to its guiding philosophy and principles. The surest way to destroy the partnership and the distinctive brand image of Saturn would be to centralize critical decisions regarding product design, component sourcing, supplier relations, manufacturing strategy, marketing, and other key processes that were heretofore within the control of Saturn leaders and their UAW partners. Without the ability to jointly influence and be held accountable for these issues, the union will cease to be in a true, full partnership, and Saturn will slowly become just another undifferentiated division of GM. In this case, what appears to be good for GM is definitely not good for Saturn. It will destroy the essence of Saturn's competitive advantage and the value Saturn adds to GM. We see this as perhaps the biggest threat facing Saturn as it moves into its second generation. How GM and Saturn address this issue will influence greatly Saturn's success.

Clearly, local and national union leaders need each other to be successful. The local needs the support of national union leaders to get the necessary resources from GM to ensure the steady flow of new products that Saturn needs to stay healthy over time. The UAW also needs Saturn to be successful and show that there is a workable alternative to both traditional adversarial relationships and nonunion outsourcing.

The new local union leaders at Saturn indicate that they are determined to achieve and maintain effective working relationships with national union leaders. The same intent and commitment are evident from national UAW leaders. The isolation of the local appears to be ending—in June 1999 a national GM-UAW plant leadership meeting was moved to Nashville for Saturn. This meeting brought together national union and corporate leaders with their counterparts from the local unions and plants that make up the GM Small Car Group. The local and national leaders have an opportunity to put this history behind them.

Reinvigorating the Shop Floor Teams and Co-Management Process

Addressing external boundary relations will need to be complemented by a number of efforts to reinvigorate internal operations. Throughout, we have emphasized that the shop floor teams and modules are the key building blocks for the rest of the organization. Unless the teams function well, Saturn cannot achieve the high level of customer satisfaction on which its past and future successes rest.

If our analysis of what drove the quality-improvement process at the module advisor level remains valid (as we believe), leading teams in a co-management structure requires high levels of communications, an alignment of views by the co-management partners, and a balance of focus between production and people issues within the teams. Reinforcing this definition of management by team leaders, module advisors, and other leaders and holding them accountable for reaching the performance targets appropriate for their units should pay significant dividends in the future, as they did in the past.

Yet we have become concerned that Saturn has drifted away from these principles in recent years. The local union's Congress, which we found to be effective in creating a dense social network and enhancing intraorganizational communications, has diminished somewhat in its importance to local union leadership, and the non-represented partners are still not involved in Congress meetings or some functional equivalent. Instead, there has been some movement to make non-represented partners more responsible for production and running the business and to have their represented counterparts focus more on people problems. This creates the kind of imbalance that our research showed leads to lower quality performance. Finally, alignment between partners requires work and time to mature. In the past few years, however, partnerships between represented and non-represented managers seem to be reorganized frequently with regard to factors other than enhancing alignment. Saturn needs to build on its past successes and pay increased attention to the principles of communication, balance, and alignment in co-management, because these have had a strong impact on past performance. This has been and can be again a major strength and key competitive advantage for Saturn.

Focusing on Continuous Improvement and Productivity

Focusing on reinvigorating the partnership at the team level would help to address two specific issues that our research indicated need improvement: off-line problem solving and productivity. The two are obviously interrelated. Off-line problem solving is an important source of continuous improvement and organizational learning. Despite the partnership and on-line team structure, Saturn has consistently experienced problems in developing a sustained off-line problem solving capability. The solution to improving off-line problem solving is relatively clear, and indeed the parties came to this solution in meetings we attended as far back as 1992. Leadership of the Manufacturing Action Council needs to focus off-line problem solving around one or two strategic issues each year, and those issues need to be ones that resonate with the rank and file and are reflected in the risk-and-reward formula. Then, the MAC has to follow up and hold teams and module advisors accountable.

Saturn has demonstrated that it can deliver world-class quality products and services to its customers, but this quality is produced at a relatively high price. Productivity has varied over time. For a while, it was high relative to other GM operations; however, in recent years it declined. When benchmarked against world-class productivity standards, however, Saturn remains far below the top tier of assembly plant operations.

Saturn does not have to be at the top of the industry in the standard productivity metric (hours per car) to be successful. As we noted in Chapter 2, Saturn was not and is not designed to meet all the principles of lean manufacturing. Instead, consistent with its stakeholder principles, its manufacturing strategy is designed to achieve multiple objectives, including productivity and costs, quality and customer satisfaction, brand image, and job security. Short-run efforts to push exclusively toward any one of these objectives might do more harm than good by undermining the trust and support of one or more key stakeholders—in this case, the work force and its union representatives. Still, some improvement in productivity is needed.

To foster continuous improvement, rank-and-file team members need to be convinced that there is a credible prospect for long-term job security at Saturn. The decision to source the SUV should provide this assurance. The second requirement, then, is to build a continuous improvement process that dovetails the on-line team process with bottom-up off-line problem solving focused on key targets chosen by the MAC leadership. Furthermore, engineering and other resources need to support cross-team problem solving as they have done so successfully in the recent launches. Finally, senior management must hold partners accountable for meeting their performance targets.

Leading a Team-Based Organization

The new leadership at Saturn needs to solve the generic paradox of leadership in a team-based culture and multi-stakeholder organization. Empowering teams at lower levels of an organization and sustaining their motivation and high performance requires leaders to provide a clear vision and sense of direction and then hold everyone accountable for meeting the responsibilities entrusted to them. Paradoxically, team-based organizations require stronger, not weaker, leaders at the top than traditional hierarchies, because in traditional hierarchies, rules govern behavior more than discretionary effort and dispersed decision making. As we have seen, finding ways to mix strong leadership and delegation of authority has been a challenge for both management and union leaders at Saturn.

Leadership at Saturn is more than the CEO. For the moment, however, we stress the challenges facing Cynthia Trudell, Saturn's current CEO. She must be a highly visible leader within Saturn and continually rebuild the trust of the union leadership and work force as someone who has a deep commitment to the vision and value of Saturn. At the same time, she must hold everyone in the organization—including herself—accountable for improving economic performance and employee morale and getting the resources needed to sustain Saturn and the careers of its employees. She must also develop a co-leadership model by working with the newly elected UAW leaders and then, by demonstrating this shared leadership style, insist that all other managers recruited to Saturn or currently in place adopt similar leadership styles. Inconsistency must be dealt with sharply and quickly, making it clear that failure to develop a shared leadership style will be fatal to a manager's career both at Saturn and within GM overall. Thus, although leadership is a shared process, leading a team-based organization requires a CEO who sets a clear vision of the future, builds commitment to strategies for achieving the vision, and holds everyone accountable for implementation.

If the stakeholder or partnership model is to survive, the leaders of the other stakeholder groups—in this case, the union leaders—must share responsibility for meeting the key challenges that face the organization. This can be successfully accomplished only through relationships built on mutual trust and aligned visions of organizational goals and the processes to achieve them. This was the lesson learned from our study of the co-management process at the module level. We believe it applies here as well. As Saturn enters its second generation, all its leaders need to work to rekindle the sense of mission and commitment among the managers, union representatives, and employees that contribute to its competitive advantage.

Managing the Effects of Union Politics

Democracy is a critical requirement for any union, but especially one that seeks to represent members in strategic decisions and corporate governance. Leaders must remain accountable to their members. The ability of the members to replace leaders who, they believe, are not representing their interests effectively or have lost touch with rank-and-file priorities must be preserved. Politics can also exert a price on operational efficiency, however. The UAW has a long and rich history of internal caucuses that vie for power. This is the UAW brand of union democracy. But it poses a tough question: Has this organized caucus system become too politicized and polarizing to be effective?

At Saturn this question converges with the question of whether the jointly selected union leaders will be replaced by others loyal to the caucus and leadership in power or whether their ability to perform the duties of these positions determines if individuals stay in these jobs. A partnership that is committed to high performance cannot afford to use key managerial jobs as political patronage positions. To do so will, in the end, reduce the respect and support that team members have for these leaders. Thus, the democratic process of replacing elected union leaders must continue while the local puts qualified and competent leaders in the partnership positions and ensures they can remain in these roles so long as they meet performance expectations.

Information-sharing and social network–building processes are critical to a modern local union. Saturn's local union leaders need to reinvigorate the many forums and means built into their organization for communicating with each other and their membership. Returning to the internal organizing processes that served the union well in the past may be helpful. This local union has been a pioneer in developing innovative communications mechanisms—the Congress, Town Hall meetings, planning and rap sessions, and member-to-member surveys to elicit rank-and-file input on priorities, intranet, and various newsletters, bulletins, and broadband—all of which helped create a dense social network among its members and leaders that clearly added value to the enterprise and the local. These need to be used to full advantage to avoid developing a leadership-membership gulf similar to the one that led to the defeat of earlier leaders. The big challenge for union leaders is to keep from getting too isolated from the membership as they engage in dialogue with management.

Encouraging External and Internal Learning and Diffusion

Saturn has not learned enough from its own successes and failures and from the successes of other benchmark operations in the automobile or other industries. The parties at Saturn allowed themselves to become isolated from the outside resources they need to survive and to adapt. Similarly, Saturn's GM and the UAW parent organizations have not learned much over the first generation of Saturn's history. This must change if the full return on the investment of these parent organizations is to be realized from this experiment.

We see the failure to learn from the experiences at Saturn as the biggest missed opportunity of the company's first generation. A diffusion strategy involving all Saturn's stakeholders—in Spring Hill, in Wilmington, and in Detroit—needs to be created to support learning from Saturn's successes and failures and for Saturn to learn from other parts of GM and the automobile industry, and from outside the automobile industry. Just as the Committee of 99 benchmarked operations inside and outside the global auto industry, so too must Saturn as it moves into its second generation. The learning council we suggested in 1993 is one way to do this. Bringing the Saturn Alumni together and fostering ongoing networks of managers from Saturn and GM is another. Clearly, other options for promoting mutual learning can be conceived and put in place. Whatever steps are taken, the key is to promote *mutual learning* so that lessons travel in both directions across these organizational boundaries.

Saturn faces a number of identifiable challenges common to labor-management partnerships. These need to be addressed as it manages its transition to its next generation. There is no guarantee that the company will be successful, but the good news is that the leaders at Saturn recognize the issues and their importance and are actively working to address them. This has been a major strength of this organization as we have observed and worked with it over the years. Because multiple stakeholders are involved in most critical management meetings, there is, as Bob McKersie noted as early as 1990, a high level of candor, an ability to face rather than avoid tough problems, and a willingness to work on them jointly. If this spirit and culture prevail, the issues can be addressed successfully, and Saturn can move forward to build its second-generation products, customer base, and partnership.

Broader Lessons

It is time to draw out the lessons of Saturn's experience for those who will shape the future of labor-management relations practices and policies and for those who will be designing and managing the organizations of the future. As social scientists, we recognize the limits of generalizing from a single case, but we see Saturn as what methodologists often refer to as a *critical case*—that is, one that brings into sharp relief a number of generic issues that others will encounter in the future, although the details of these future cases may not mirror those at Saturn.

The key to effective transfer of learning, as much organizational theory tells us, is not to attempt to imitate other's practices, but to engage in an *adaptive learning* process.[1] Adaptive learning begins with a clear understanding of the problem one's own organization is trying to solve. With Saturn's Committee of 99, the problem was defined clearly—figure out how to build a small car profitably with U.S. workers and UAW representation. The second step is to study intensively how someone else's benchmark or potentially useful practice works well in the institutional setting and environment in which it is located. Again, using the Saturn example, one might need to look carefully at what makes Saturn's on-line teams work well and how they have been supported by the role of the union and the broader partnership. With this *deep understanding*, the parties involved can discuss how to adapt the key lessons from the benchmark practice or organization to fit into their home environment and institutional setting. Experimentation and learning can then begin with full recognition that no set of practices can be adopted without making adjustments to related organizational practices or institutions. Over time, what tends to evolve is not an imitation of the benchmark practice, but yet another innovation that may change the home institutions in an evolutionary and informed fashion. It is with this adaptive learning model in mind that we offer broader implications of this case.

Labor-Management Practices and Policies

Labor-Management Partnerships

It is important to recognize the Saturn model is not the one best alternative to traditional labor-management relations. The world of labor relations is far too varied for any single model to fit all circumstances, now or in the future. Not all labor or management leaders are comfortable with or capable of building and working with the full-scale partnership found at Saturn. Moreover, in settings in which the boundary of a single enterprise is highly uncertain, partnerships built on a single-enterprise model are not likely to be effective or stable. In these settings, cross-firm networks or other institutional arrangements are likely to be better suited.[2]

Although the partnership structure used at Saturn was well suited to the history and particular circumstances of the UAW and GM in the mid-1980s, this is not the only model for labor-management partnerships in which a single-company partnership does appear to make sense. Indeed, we have come to believe that it is less the formal structures that are the essence of the partnership than the key processes that underlie the structures. The structures help but are the wrong elements to focus on in learning from this experience. What is required is a new set of skills and capabilities on the part of both labor and management representatives. Labor representatives need the knowledge and skills to add value in making and implementing strategic and operational decisions. They need to be willing to be held accountable for decisions reached on a shared basis. At the same time, they must balance their roles as partners with managers with their roles as democratically elected leaders with defined constituencies and independent resources and power. Ultimately, the challenge for union leaders in the future is to achieve and maintain a workable balance across these different roles.

Managers also need to find and maintain a similar balance between representing the interests of the enterprise and the owners or other top executives to whom they are accountable, working as partners with union leaders, and advocating for the resources and organizational supports needed to sustain the partnership. Labor-management partnerships are, and for the foreseeable future will be, highly controversial within management circles. Sharing power with union leaders is not a well-accepted principle. Managers who have had little exposure to labor relations or human resource management will not take naturally to their roles as partners. They need training to do so, and their rewards and career prospects need to be contingent on their success as partners. As managers come and go, so too will support for partnership principles, unless the organization has a conscious strategy and plan for management succession and placement and that plan includes a requirement that new managers support and get the necessary training to manage as partners.

We cannot overemphasize these last two points. American labor and management have built up a deep and powerful culture of adversarialism in union-management relationships that, if anything, has become more strongly embedded in recent years as fewer managers have direct contact or exposure to labor leaders. In the absence of direct evidence from personal experience, general stereotypes dominate cultural attitudes of management toward labor and labor toward management. Only by confronting this issue directly will these stereotypes be overcome.

Unions and Their Leaders

Saturn demonstrates that there is a new source of power available to local unions today. In knowledge-driven enterprises, unions and their members can gain power not just by their threatening to withhold labor but also by adding value to the work process and to the products and services delivered to customers. Learning how to organize members to ensure they are sources of value added, and then using this source of power and value to achieve mutual gains for the enterprise and the work force, are critical roles for the union leaders of the future. This requires that leaders balance new co-management skills with the political skills required of any democratically elected leader and with a concern for individual representation.

Clearly, centralization of power and decision making in national unions is being challenged by the need for greater flexibility of local unions to adapt practices to fit their members' preferences and the local employer's needs. This cannot be done in a vacuum, however, because national union leaders need to guard against a slow degradation of industry standards and be ready and able to negotiate for resources controlled by corporate decision makers. Moreover, national union leaders need to be facilitators and catalysts for learning and innovation across locals. Just as the local at Saturn derived considerable power from the expertise its members and leaders built through participation in business decision making, so too can national union leaders add value and derive power by promoting learning from one local to another, within and across firms, and by using the knowledge gained and value added through this experience to hold corporate decision makers accountable. Although this is not a substitute for bargaining power achieved through centralized collective bargaining, it can be a complementary source of power that national unions will need to capture if they are to add value to their members and to American industry and society in the future.

The fact that unions take on broader functions does not mean that collective bargaining becomes less important. Bargaining with a clear deadline sometimes is needed to resolve tough issues, as was the case at Saturn in 1998 and 1999. The art of balancing bargaining and participatory strategies lies in knowing how to use the mix of interest-based and traditional power-based techniques in negotiations.[3] With this knowledge at hand, the problem-solving and analytical skills from ongoing participation and the information about how the business operates can be used constructively in negotiations. There is widespread awareness and use of these techniques in collective bargaining today.[4] Union leaders need to be trained in these techniques and then add them, as appropriate, to their tool kit for representing members. At the same time, unions (and management) need to retain their ability to draw the line in negotiations when differences persist on a key bargaining issue. It is naïve to expect that conflict goes away in a labor-management partnership or stakeholder organization. The key challenge for stakeholder organizations lies in effectively managing and resolving the conflicts that are sure to surface.

Labor Relations Managers and Corporate Executives

The vision and competitive pressures that led GM leaders to create and support Saturn in the mid-1980s diminished as these leaders retired.

Their successors defined GM's competitive threats as coming from other sources—the company's high costs could be reduced better by accelerating and expanding outsourcing; duplication of brands and platforms could be addressed by integrating and centralizing design, engineering, and component sourcing; and labor relations could be changed only by taking on the UAW in traditional, adversarial bargaining. Rather than hold everyone's feet to the fire by driving continuous improvements through innovations in shop floor relations and production systems, GM, like other U.S. automakers, shifted their focus to getting high volume and hot-selling trucks, SUVs, and other bigger models out the door in large numbers. Such is the half-life of the vision and strategy that drive most U.S. companies. The question is whether the centralizing, outsourcing, downsizing, and return to hard-line bargaining have now about run their course at GM and other U.S. firms. At some point, the seesawing of American management with respect to labor-management relations needs to give way to a more consistent, long-term vision and strategy that have a life beyond the tenure of any single CEO or top management team. Indeed, this is a key reason why Ford is often described as having a better and more productive relationship with the UAW than GM. Ford's vision and strategy have been stable and consistent for nearly two decades. This is an important lesson, not only for GM and other auto companies, but also for leaders across American industry.

Disseminating the lessons of Saturn has been difficult for GM. One reason for this is quite simple: no one saw it as his or her responsibility to design and implement a learning process that linked the innovative unit to the rest of the organization. As a result, the inevitable isolation set in. Managers who want to reap the full reward from their investment in innovation need to manage the learning process as well. Although protecting the autonomy of an innovative experiment may be important in the early years, isolation has enormous costs over time, as Saturn's experience illustrates. The advances of modern communications' technologies make it much easier to share information quickly and to build dense communications networks among employees and managers across units and, indeed, between industry and research and educational institutions. The current buzzword for this is "knowledge management." The managers who go beyond the buzzword and figure out how to leverage the knowledge gained from experimentation and innovation by building processes for shared learning through personal and technology-mediated interactions will be the true knowledge managers and their organizations will be truly learning organizations. The key lesson from Saturn is that going beyond the buzzwords requires a conscious commitment of resources and leadership to make it happen.

Labor Relations Policy Makers

Those of us who are committed to updating our policies, institutions, and practices to fit today's economy and work force should recognize Saturn for what it is: the boldest labor relations experiment in the country, one that is unique. It provides a window on how a radically different model might work. The most interesting and innovative part of the Saturn model we observed was not the formal labor-management committees or joint consultative and decision-making bodies, but the one-on-one partnering we call *co-management*. It is apparent that union leaders carry out functions that traditional labor and employment laws would define as managerial. The ironic twist is that if current labor law were to be applied to these co-managers, they would be reclassified as exempt from wage and hour standards and ruled to be ineligible for union membership! Such is the outmoded nature of America's labor and employment laws—regulations passed and carried over from an image of how work was done and organizational roles were written in the industrial age of the 1930s.

Clearly, although Saturn may be the extreme example of an organization that violates both sets of laws in this manner, it is far from alone. Across America, we continuously see examples of "hourly" workers and union representatives engaging in decisions regarding work force allocation, customer service, product development, process control, product quality, production scheduling, suppliers, and outsourcing. They travel together to learn about new technologies or work practices, visit customers, or gather other information relevant to future decisions. Firms are constantly advised by consultants, the business press, and business school faculty to share more managerial information and bring frontline workers into decisions about how to do their jobs, organize work, and manage their work groups. It is time to bring labor and employment law into better conformance with sensible contemporary work and organizational practices. No worker should lose his or her right to union representation for having taken on these managerial duties and responsibilities.

Saturn was designed from day one as a joint labor-management project. GM therefore agreed to extend recognition to the UAW on a voluntary basis. The innovations in work design, employee participation, and union-management relations implemented would not have been possible had the traditional approach to organizing a new facility been followed. If management had set up its own greenfield site and resisted union-organizing efforts, both sides would have devoted resources to the organizing and counter-organizing campaign, and even if the union succeeded in winning a contested election, the seeds of an adversarial relationship would already have taken root.

Our labor law puts on, at best, murky legal footing any joint design and extension of union recognition that takes place before the recruitment of a work force. Instead, it encourages a battle for the loyalty and support of the work force in the name of a union representation election campaign. A number of other companies and unions in the steel, telecommunications, office products, and other industries have recognized the disadvantages of an adversarial battle over union recognition, particularly in settings in which a company expands its operations by opening a new facility or line of business. These are still the exceptions to the general rule, however, and nothing in our national labor policy encourages or supports these efforts. It is clearly in the national interest to promote these more cooperative, nonadversarial approaches to this process.

This last point suggests that the role of the government in employment relations must be to do more than enforce rules. Government leaders must also be champions and catalysts for innovation and learning. The nation has a big stake in learning the right lessons from Saturn and from other innovations and in encouraging labor and management to adapt them in ways that fit their particular needs. As early as the mid-1980s, it was becoming clear that traditional labor-management relations needed to change to support more direct employee participation, workplace flexibility, and information sharing, and a greater worker voice in the higher level decisions that shape the long-term futures of the enterprise and the work force. If anything, that need is greater today than before. The sad fact is that nearly twenty years after the ideas that led to Saturn were first discussed, it remains the most radical and forward-looking labor-management innovation in America. No other contenders for this perhaps unenviable position have emerged since then, and the pace of innovations of less substantial magnitude has likewise slowed. The commitment to innovation in labor-management relations needs to be rekindled. Government leaders can no longer afford to remain passive observers of the slow atrophy of collective bargaining and union membership in the country. This does not mean, however, that we are urging a return to big government or more centralized direction of the economy or labor relations. Instead, government must become a catalyst for sensible innovations by learning through research and experimentation what works at the local level, using the same communications and network-building tools to disseminate the lessons learned from these innovations, and providing resources to build the institutional capacities (e.g., new union leadership skills) needed for these innovations to spread. This can be done only if the American public insists on putting the future of work on the national agenda, where it belongs.

Organizations of the Future

Saturn is not modeled on lean production. Instead, it was designed to achieve multiple objectives, which include but are not limited to lean principles. Saturn was designed to address both shareholders' interests for a profitable small car and labor's interests in jobs and union representation. Those who shaped the original design and those who adapted it over time and in practice put these broad objectives into operation by focusing on multiple metrics of cost, quality and customer satisfaction, brand image, and job security. Although in the best of all possible worlds these objectives might be mutually reinforcing or complementary, from time to time they are likely to require some tough trade-offs, at least in the short run. This was clearly the case when the market for small cars softened and short-term productivity and costs became trade-off issues with employment continuity.

One need not buy into the full Saturn organizational model to extract useful lessons for organizational design, however. We focus on three issues that organizational designers face today: (1) whether and how to build effective teams or, more specifically, teamwork, (2) how to gain the flexibility and advantages of a highly networked organization, and (3) whether and how to build multiple stakeholder principles into the design and governance processes of future organizations.

Team-Based Organizations

What made Saturn's frontline teams work well, and what lessons might the answer offer those who will be designing and managing future organizations that rely heavily on teams?[5] Saturn developed outstanding capabilities to control processes and solve problems within its teams, as well as a dense communication network that resolved problems between units, because both the company and the union were committed to quality and possessed the knowledge and organizational resources needed to make the production process work. Knowledge about what needed to be done to serve the customer was widely diffused through the organization. What is most impressive, and what we believe is generalizable, is the ongoing, on-line self-direction, problem solving, and responsibility of the teams; the co-management and coordination by the module advisors; and the responsibility for quality taken on by the union.

We start with the basics—the workers (team members) themselves. Saturn has indeed made knowledge workers out of its shop floor production workers. They are superbly trained and know how to build cars. The initial work force was selected carefully for its commitment to quality and teamwork. Initial and ongoing training and information sharing emphasized the dignity and pride of the workers on the front lines. Saturn's early advertising showed team members at work, solving problems and going the extra mile to serve customers. The "Different Kind of Company" slogan signaled to the public and the organization that the team members were important. Communicating internally and externally that the work force was a core competency that came with the product worked well for Saturn, particularly in its early years. Creating this excitement and culture, grounded in real knowledge, skills, and information sharing, is, we believe, a necessary starting point for any organization that is serious about making its full work force and teamwork competitive assets.

This initial excitement and level of shared knowledge are difficult to maintain over time. They require constant maintenance and periodic reinvigoration. The key is to keep team members and leaders from losing faith in the competence and commitment of the higher-level managers and union leaders who are expected to attend to the long-term viability of the enterprise and business. A key task of leaders of a team-based organization is to maintain the trust and confidence of the team members. This means providing strategic leadership that safeguards the long-term viability and employment security of the enterprise and work force and providing an internal management system that supports and supplements the work of the teams. Leading a team-based organization is a considerable challenge for management and union leaders. Team members who are well informed will be more critical of management and have higher expectations for management performance than workers in traditionally structured and managed organizations.

The Saturn case also offers a caution regarding the overuse of teams as a panacea for all the problems of traditional management structures or work organization systems. The key roles that the module advisors (i.e., supervisors) play at Saturn as problem solvers, lateral and vertical communication links, and expert resources drive home two important points. First, there is no such thing as an autonomous work team in highly interdependent production or service organizations, and therefore teams must be linked and coordinated.[6] Supervisors, team leaders, module advisors—call them what you will, they continue to play critical roles in organizations. Decentralizing more decision making to team members may reduce the number of supervisors needed, but the critical linking, coordinating, and leading functions they serve do not disappear. The key organizational design and management task is to develop and reward supervisors so that they are both effective facilitators and coaches for team members and proactive managers of their external boundaries, a point on which we will elaborate more fully.

Second, *teamwork*, not structures, is what matters. The key contributions that Saturn's teams (and teams in any other organization) make are to enable rapid coordination and enhance problem solving on a continuous and, as needed, periodic basis. Teams can do so if they bring grounded and diverse expertise to bear on a problem and can act quickly to implement ideas that have merit. There is no one best way to achieve these capabilities, and team structures are perhaps only one of a variety of ways to do so. Just as tight job descriptions and specialization worked well in the early days of mass production and then became problematic and overly rigid, so too might specific team structures atrophy over time and need to be shaken up and recharged. Keeping an eye on the processes teams are expected to generate, rather than on their more visible structural elements, is critical to using teams sensibly.

Our network analysis findings suggest that a key to achieving positive performance results from teams lies in managing their external boundaries.[7] Thus, we see an important role for teams, and particularly for team leaders, in organizations that seek to create strong network ties across individuals and groups. The team leader's critical tasks are to find ways to foster high levels of lateral communication and coordination among teams and to maintain a clear balance between meeting the needs of the people in their teams and addressing production and quality problems. Moreover, if these tasks are co-managed either by creating formal co-management roles, as at Saturn, or informally as union representatives or workers themselves take on more managerial responsibilities, the views of these co-managers need to be aligned, and they need to balance their responsibilities for addressing people and production issues rather than specialize in one or the other.

An important key implication for team-based organizations in general is that management can no longer be set apart as a separate function assigned to a separate class of employees. Instead, it becomes a function that is shared more widely across all levels of the organization. Accepting this principle requires a cultural and, to some extent, an ideological shift for some managers and some union leaders. Unless the parties are prepared to make this shift, it is probably better not to try making teams a central core competency or source of competitive advantage, because eventually the teams will collapse or lose their effectiveness.

Networked Organizations

The implications of our analysis for organizations that require high levels of lateral communications, coordination, and rapid on-line problem solving are straightforward. Allow multiple opportunities for social and task-related interactions to develop among individuals and groups that would not normally interact if traditional bureaucratic rules or hierarchical reporting structures prevail. Indeed, the development of the dense communications patterns we observed among union-represented and non-represented managers at Saturn is one of the most interesting and positive, but unanticipated, consequences of the labor-management partnership. In traditional labor relations, communications channels are highly formalized and limited. CEOs and other line managers in particular are protected from direct contact with union leaders by their labor relations professionals. If problems cannot be resolved informally, supervisors are expected to refer them to formal grievance procedure representatives, as are their union counterparts. But as the labor-management partnership model took shape in practice, the co-management process and the local union's ongoing efforts to "organize" its members created multiple arenas and forums in which union representatives interacted with line managers and high-level executives. Elected officers and union members with leadership positions in the partnership met with each other regularly in the various internal union meetings (e.g., Congress) and political events, and information flowed across boundaries based on understanding of who was in the know. Opening up to these more fluid opportunities for interaction for social, political, and task-related functions is what made Saturn—and what could make other organizations—truly networked-based organizations.

Opportunities for interaction are, however, only a necessary and not sufficient condition to build the level of trust needed to foster value-added communications. More frequent interaction among individuals or groups who see their interests as diametrically opposed only creates new venues for battle. At the other extreme, parties need not have totally common goals and interests to benefit from interactions. Trust and personal relationships instead require respect for each other and acceptance of the legitimacy of others' interests, even if they are not shared. Indeed, one of the long-standing lessons of labor-management relations is that effective negotiators build trust with each other by respecting the legitimacy of the other's needs and building the personal relationships needed to talk off the record about options for reaching agreements that both sides can accept. This kind of trust requires some shared values and understanding of the task at hand and the other's point of view. In the network analysis of module advisors at Saturn, we described this as an alignment between the represented and non-represented partners on the tasks, priorities, and jobs they shared. At Saturn, quality and customer satisfaction were the shared values that produced a sufficient sense of common purpose among the different parties. They could disagree on other issues, such as how to structure the risk-and-reward plan or how to rebalance the tasks assigned to different work units on the assembly line, but quality and customer satisfaction remained shared values around which all could coalesce. The best evidence was the black arm-band incident in 1993 during which union members believed that it was okay to protest publicly what they believed was a weakening of management's commitment to quality. Management, in turn, was deeply hurt that its commitment to this organizational value would be questioned. The result was that both sides cleared the air and refocused their energies around this core value.

Thus, Saturn illustrates how a networked organization can evolve in an environment in which, while the parties recognize the need to address both their common and their conflicting objectives, they build trust and personal relationships that can be drawn on as social capital in times of crisis or in the daily routine of solving problems. This level of trust must be earned over time; it cannot be forced or required from the top down. Networked organizations evolve out of shared experiences and interactions and can be nurtured, but not commanded, from above.

Organizational Governance and Stakeholder Relations

Long ago, organization theorists came to the conclusion there is no one best way to structure and govern organizations. Yet the business press, management lobbyists, and most policy makers cling to the view that the primary, if not the sole, purpose of American corporations should be to maximize shareholder wealth. Perhaps it is time to confront this issue and challenge this prevailing view by encouraging organizational forms that provide other stakeholders a voice in the critical decisions that affect their "investments."[8] There is no single best way to do this any more than there is a single best way to manage corporations today. There are, however, few empirical studies or critical examinations of such firms in action. Saturn serves as a critical case of a stakeholder firm in action, one worthy of understanding and further tracking as it moves through its second generation.

We draw three broader theoretical and policy implications from our study of Saturn as one prototype of a stakeholder firm.[9] First, it became a stakeholder firm designed to serve multiple interests (job creation, learning laboratory, and production and marketing of a small car with high customer enthusiasm) because parties with these multiple interests participated in the design of the organization from its inception. It would not have taken this organizational form or accepted the mission it did if its design had been left to one interested party—that is, management. The Committee of 99 clearly had an effect on the goals and mission of the organization. Too much of the research and policy writing about stakeholder organizations simply pleads with managers to be more responsive to different stakeholders. If our analysis is at all generalizable, it challenges that narrow managerial approach to the design of this type of organization.

Second, two processes were identified in our analysis as critical for the performance of Saturn as a stakeholder firm. The first was its ability to develop effective network relationships across the key stakeholders. To date, most studies of networked organizations and stakeholder organizations have proceeded on parallel, but separate, tracks. This case suggests that they are interrelated in a complementary way and should be considered together by those who study and those who will be designing the organizations of the future. The second process was the ability to confront and then resolve conflicts. Clearly, conflict resolution is an important function in any organization, but in an organization that by design brings multiple interests into its mission and governance processes, we suggest that conflict resolution becomes *the* critical function. If the different interests at stake cannot be addressed effectively and efficiently, stakeholder firms will suffocate under their own weight. Developing the capacity to resolve conflicts is a critical managerial skill for those who will shape these types of organizations in the future.

Third, for stakeholder firms similar to Saturn to survive over time and grow in number, the ideologies of key groups in society must change significantly. It was not just executives at GM or top leaders of the UAW who were critical of their predecessors' decision to set up Saturn on a stakeholder model. Their criticisms were shared by many other leaders in the management, financial, and public policy communities and by some in the labor movement. Stakeholder models challenge deeply held prevailing notions about the role and power of management, the primacy of financial capital as a resource for the firm, and the role that human capital should play in the organizations of the future. For stakeholder firms to survive and grow in number requires not only must they prove themselves to be successful in carrying out their multiple goals and stated missions, but also they must be able to overcome a great deal of resistance from powerful forces.

Ultimately, public corporations are institutions that must serve society. We have an open mind as to whether shareholder-maximizing models are the best way for corporations to serve society in the future or whether society might be better served if corporations were held directly accountable to other stakeholders as well. Others should also keep an open mind on these issues. Corporate governance theorists and policy makers need to encourage more firms to assume the features of a stakeholder firm and then learn from their experiences. In our opinion, the pendulum has swung too far in the direction of meeting shareholder demands for short-term results at the expense of employees and perhaps other stakeholders. How to find a better balance among these stakeholders is likely to be a major source of public debate in the years ahead.[10]

Looking Ahead

We hope that by telling the Saturn story, the lessons from experience with this remarkable organization will help to stimulate and inform debates about the future of labor-management relations and organizational design and governance. In particular, Saturn has much to teach us about the impact that union-organized communication networks can have on performance; the possibilities for co-management; the changing nature of local unions that engage in partnerships; and the difficulties of sustaining innovation and learning within large, complex organizations. Although our data described in detail Saturn's problems as well as achievements, we remain optimistic about its future. We hope that the lessons and actions discussed here ensure that Saturn's story will, in the end, be a positive one.

Notes

1. What's at Stake Here?

1. The classic argument for the shareholder view of the firm can be found in Milton Friedman, "The Social Responsibility of Business Is to Increase Its Profits," *The New York Times Magazine* (September 13, 1970). For a more recent statement of this view, see Michael C. Jensen, "Eclipse of the Public Corporation," *Harvard Business Review*, 89 (1989): 61–74. For statements supporting a stakeholder view of the firm see R.E. Freeman, *Strategic Management: A Stakeholder Approach* (Boston: Pitman, 1984). More recent reviews of stakeholder theory can be found in two special journal issues: *Business Ethics Quarterly* 4 (1994) and *Academy of Management Journal* 42 (December 1999).

2. Thomas A. Kochan, Harry C. Katz, and Robert B. McKersie, *The Transformation of American Industrial Relations* (Ithaca, NY: Cornell University/ILR Press, 1994).

3. See Fred Foulkes, *Personnel Policies in Large Nonunion Companies* (Englewood Cliffs, N.J.: Prentice Hall, 1980) or John J. Lawler, *Unionization and Deunionization: Strategy, Tactics, and Outcomes* (Columbia, S.C.: University of South Carolina Press, 1990).

4. For an expression of this view particularly focused on the auto industry and its labor relations, see Mike Parker and Jane Slaughter, *Choosing Sides* (Boston: South End Press, 1988).

5. For a review of the unsuccessful efforts to update and reform labor law see the symposium devoted to discussion of the Report of the Commission on the Future of Worker Management Relations found in *Industrial Relations* 34, 3 (1995). For an equally unsuccessful effort to initiate a debate over the corporation as a "citizen" in society, see Robert B. Reich, *The New Corporate Citizenship* (Washington, D.C: U.S. Department of Labor, April 16, 1996).

6. See Kochan, et al., *The Transformation of American Industrial Relations*.

7. For thorough description of the developments in the auto industry in the 1980s see Harry C. Katz, *Shifting Gears* (Cambridge, Mass.: MIT Press, 1985).

8. For a review of the evidence of increasing shareholder activism in the 1980s and 1990s see Michael Useem, *Investor Capitalism* (New York: Basic Books, 1996).

9. An interesting account of this set of issues is found in a book written by the former chief economist at General Motors. See Maria von Neuman Whitman, *New World, New Rules* (Boston: Harvard Business School Press, 1999). See also Thomas A. Kochan, "Rebuilding the Social Contract at Work: A Call to Action," Presidential Address to the 52nd Annual Meetings of the Industrial Relations Research Association, January 2000, reprinted in *Perspectives on Work* 4, 1 (2000).

10. See, for example, Wayne Baker, "The Network Organization in Theory and Practice." In *Networks and Organizations: Structure, Form, and Action*, edited by Nitin Nohria and Robert Eccles (Boston: Harvard Business School Press, 1992), 397–429.

11. For discussion of the role of social capital in networks see Ronald S. Burt, *Structural Holes* (Cambridge, Mass.: Harvard University Press, 1992) or Masahiko Aoki, "Toward an Economic Model of the Japanese Firm," *Journal of Economic Literature* 27 (March 1990): 1–27.

12. For a recent statement in support of this view by a group of high level business and labor leaders in America see "The Principles for New Employment Relationships: A Report from the Collective Bargaining Forum," *Perspectives on Work* 3 (1999): 32–39.

2. Walter Reuther's Legacy: The Ideas behind Saturn

1. For a good historical account of these negotiations see Nelson Lichtenstein, *The Most Dangerous Man in Detroit* (New York: Basic Books, 1995).

2. Barry Bluestone and Irving Bluestone, *Negotiating for the Future* (New York: Basic Books, 1992), 52–53.

3. Louis E. Davis and Albert B. Cherns, *The Quality of Working Life* (New York: The Free Press, 1975).

4. For a discussion of the Tarrytown case, see Robert H. Guest, *Innovative Work Practices* (New York: Pergamon Press, 1982). Saul's father, Sidney P. Rubinstein, was the consultant hired by GM and the UAW to design and implement the first QWL effort at Tarrytown.

5. Harry C. Katz, Thomas A. Kochan, and Kenneth Gobeille, "Industrial Relations Performance, Economic Performance and QWL," *Industrial and Labor Relations Review* 37 (1983): 3–17.

6. See John Krafcik, "Triumph of the Lean Production System," *Sloan Management Review* 30, 1, Fall (1988) and John Paul MacDuffie, "Human Resource Bundles and Manufacturing Performance: Organizational Logic and Production Systems in the World Auto Industry," *Industrial and Labor Relations Review* 48 (1995): 197–221.

7. NUMMI has also been thoroughly studied by academic researchers. See, for example, Paul Adler, "The Learning Bureaucracy: The New United Motors Manufacturing Inc." In *Research in Organizational Behavior, Volume 15*, edited by Larry L. Cummings and Barry M. Staw (Greenwich, Conn.: JAI Press, 1992), 180–205; Welford Wilms, *Restoring Prosperity: How Workers and Managers are Forging a New*

Culture of Cooperation (New York: Times Business, 1996); or David I. Levine, *Reinventing the Workplace* (Washington, D.C.: The Brookings Institution, 1995).

8. Adler, "The Learning Bureaucracy."

9. For a firsthand account of the work of the Committee of 99 see Jack O'Toole, *Forming the Future: Lessons from the Saturn Corporation* (Cambridge, Mass.: Blackwell Publishers, 1996).

10. O'Toole, pp. 16–20.

11. Interviews with General Motors human resources management from the Saginaw and Inland Fisher Guide divisions, December 1992.

12. Interview with Buzz Wilms, UCLA, December 11, 1992.

13. Memorandum of Agreement, op cit.

14. J. Chris Koenders and Wujin Chu, "A Case Study of Saturn's Distribution Strategy," MIT International Motor Vehicle Program Working Paper, April 1993, 38–39.

15. James Womack, Daniel Jones, and Daniel Roos, *The Machine That Changed the World.* (New York: Rawson, 1990).

16. For our own theoretical analysis of the principles of a stakeholder firm see Thomas A. Kochan and Saul Rubinstein, "Toward a Stakeholder Theory of the Firm: The Saturn Partnership," *Organization Science* 11 (July/August, 2000): 367–386.

3. The Partnership in Action

1. J.D. Power & Associates. 1992, 1993, 1994, 1995, 1996, 1997, 1998. *Customer Satisfaction Index.* Agoura Hills, Calif.

2. *The Harbour Report.* Harbour and Associates, Detroit, 1995, 1999.

3. The full quantitative analysis, for those interested in the technical details, can be found in Saul Rubinstein, "The Impact of Co-Management on Quality Performance: The Case of the Saturn Corporation," *Industrial and Labor Relations Review* 53 (January 2000): 197–218.

4. Reinventing the Local Union

1. See Sumner Slichter, *Union Policies and Industrial Management* (Washington, D.C.: The Brookings Institution, 1941); Clinton S. Golden and Harold J. Ruttenberg, *The Dynamics of Industrial Democracy* (New York: Harper and Brothers, 1942).

2. Michael Bennett, "New Roles for Unions in a Team Environment," Work In America Productivity Forum, Manuscript, 1988.

3. Joel Cutcher-Gershenfeld, Robert McKersie, and Kirsten Wever, *The Changing Role of Union Leaders* (Washington, D.C.: US Department of Labor, Bureau of Labor-Management Cooperation, U.S. Government Printing Office, 1988).

4. See, for example, Louis A. Ferman, Michele Hoyman, Joel Cutcher-Gershenfeld, and Ernest J. Savoie, eds., *Joint Training Programs: A Union-Management Approach to Preparing Workers for the Future* (Ithaca, N.Y.: ILR Press, 1991).

5. For a discussion of these generic tensions, see Harry Katz and Charles Sabel, "Industrial Relations and Industrial Adjustment in the Car Industry," *Industrial Relations* 24 (1985): 295–315.

6. "Labor's Days at GM," *The Wall Street Journal* (September 4, 1992): A8.

5. Boundary Management and Learning Disabilities

1. "Saturn," *Business Week* (August 17, 1992): 86.

2. "Can Detroit Make Cars That Baby Boomers Like?" *Business Week* (December 1, 1997): 144.

3. Arthur Stinchcombe, "Social Structure and Organizations." In *Handbook of Organizations*, edited by James G. March (Chicago: Rand-McNally, 1965), 142–193.

4. Bob Hancke and Saul Rubinstein, "Limits to Innovation in Work Organization?" In *Enriching Production*, edited by Ake Sandberg (Aldershot, England: Avebury Press, 1995), 179–198.

5. Reuters, July 20, 1995.

6. For a business school case that outlines the pros and cons of these different options, complete with estimates of their costs and profits, see Arnoldo Hax, "Saturn Corporation's Module II Decision," Harvard Business School Case 9-795011 (August 18, 1994).

7. Charlene Solomon, "Behind the Wheel at Saturn," *Personnel Journal* (June 1991).

8. John Paul MacDuffie, "The Transfer of Organizing Principles: Cross-Cultural Influences on Replication at Opel Eisenach." In *Organizational and Technological Innovation in the Automotive Industry: Recent Developments*, edited by Anna Comacchio, Giuseppe Volpato, and Arnaldo Camuffo (Berlin: Springer-Verlag), 119–137 (1999).

9. For a classic discussion of the problem of diffusing innovations from greenfield sites see Richard E. Walton, "Work Innovations in the United States," *Harvard Business Review* 57 (1979): 88–98.

10. Fritz Pils and John Paul MacDuffie, "The Adoption of High-Involvement Work Practices," *Industrial Relations* 35 (1996): 423–455.

6. What Have We Learned?

1. See for example, Robert E. Cole, *Strategies for Learning: Small-Group Activities in American, Japanese, and Swedish Industry.* (Berkeley, Calif.: University of California Press, 1989); D. Eleanor Westney, *Imitation and Innovation: The Transfer of Western Organizational Patterns to Meji Japan* (Cambridge, Mass.: Harvard University Press, 1987); or Peter Senge, *The Fifth Discipline* (New York: Doubleday, 1990).

2. For a discussion of the limitations of partnerships in settings where an organization's boundary is uncertain see Saul Rubinstein and Charles Heckscher, "Labor Management Partnerships: Two Views." In *Negotiations and Change: From the Workplace to Society*, edited by Thomas A. Kochan and David B. Lipsky (Boston: MIT Sloan School of Management, 2000). Unpublished manuscript.

3. See Roger Fisher and William Ury, *Getting to Yes*, (Boston: Houghton Mifflin, 1981); Charles Heckscher and Lavinia Hall, "Mutual Gains and Beyond: Two Levels of Intervention," *Negotiations Journal* 10 (1994): 235–248; or Ann Martin, "Interest Based Bargaining: What We're Learning," *Perspectives on Work* 1 (1997): 49–53.

4. Joel Cutcher Gershenfeld, "Is Collective Bargaining Ready for the Knowledge-Driven Economy?" *Perspectives on Work* 3 (1999): 20–24.

5. For a good primer on effective team processes see Leigh Thompson, *Making the Team* (Upper Saddle River, N.J.: Prentice Hall, 2000).

6. Janice A. Klein, "Maintaining Expertise in Multi-skilled Teams." In *Theories of Self-Managed Work Teams: Volume 1*, edited by M. Beyerlein and D. Johnson (Greenwich, Conn.: JAI Press, 1994), 145–165.

7. A good discussion of the external "boundary management" roles of team leaders is found in Deborah G. Ancona, "Outward Bound: Strategies for Team Survival in an Organization," *Academy of Management Journal* 33 (1990): 334–365.

8. See Margaret Blair, *Ownership and Control* (Washington D.C.: The Brookings Institution, 1994). For a discussion of the role of stakeholders and the role of international financial institutions, see Joseph P. Stiglitz, "Toward a Democratic Model of Development," *Perspectives on Work* 4 (2000): 31–37.

9. For our own theoretical analysis of Saturn as a stakeholder firm see Thomas A. Kochan and Saul Rubinstein, "Toward a Stakeholder Theory of the Firm: The Saturn Partnership," *Organization Science* 11 (July/August, 2000): 367–386.

10. See, for example, "Hey, What about Us?" *Business Week* (December 27, 1999): 52–55.

Index

Note: Page numbers followed by *f* indicate figures; numbers followed by *t* indicate tables.

Thomas A. Kochan is the George M. Bunker Professor of Work and Employment Relations at Massachusetts Institute of Technology's Sloan School of Management.

Saul A. Rubinstein is Assistant Professor in the School of Management and Labor Relations at Rutgers University.